MTIV PROCESS, INSPIRATION AND PRACTICE FOR THE NEW MEDIA DESIGNER

BY HILLMAN CURTIS

201 WEST 103RD STREET

INDIANAPOLIS, INDIANA 46290

TABLE OF CONTENTS

SOMETIMES I brew up a double espresso, from extra strong beans that I get from the Soma Café whenever I am in San Francisco. I shoot it back and go to Apple.com/quicktime and watch movie trailers. Sad, right? Here's the really sad part… sometimes I get choked up watching them. I can't help it. It's that combination of music and motion, color and text. The quick bursts of action or slow swell of drama and the wonder of the actors. It's the way the story is laid out in front of me… usually a story I can predict if I want to. Definitely a theme.

And as a New Media designer I am looking at everything. I am looking at the quality of compression on the spot. How well it streams over the Web. I am looking at how the editor paced the trailer. I am looking at the colors the art director has chosen and how the cinematographer lit the shots. I stop the trailer at random spots and look at the composition of the shot. I always ask myself how and if these things support the story and more specifically if they support the theme. And I usually end up asking myself how can people be so smart. So talented. Able to combine bits of motion, color, music, and text to create a thirty- to sixty-second story.

And then I make my notes. I list techniques and ideas that I might be able to use later. If the trailer is especially good, I download it to a folder called motion_inspiration on my hard drive. Often when I start a project, I will transfer a trailer into our project folders and refer to it while concepting and designing.

I am not telling you this to encourage you to visit Apple.com/quicktime. I am telling you this because I want to tell you about this book, and how the story above sums it up.

I believe in New Media design. I believe in its vitality, its power, and its potential to communicate both literally and emotionally. In the right hands, even a trailer for a cheesy movie can inspire. This book, which I've divided into three sections — Process, Inspiration, and Practice — is my way of sharing not only what I have learned designing New Media, but also the deep respect I have for this vital and important discipline.

WHAT'S NEW MEDIA DESIGN? New Media is anything that is digital and plays on a screen.

The New Media designer is anyone practicing digital design. I also believe that a majority of New Media designers, like me, have reinvented themselves in this field... perhaps coming from a background not defined by design or design school. A person looking for ways to grow with this new field.

WHAT IS "MAKING THE INVISIBLE VISIBLE"? When I was 12 years old I regularly raided my stepfather, Paul's, book collection. I would grab the poster books. Most of them were books on the propaganda posters of the Second World War. I was fascinated by the type, layout, and powerful juxtaposition of deep reds with heavy blacks, luminous bronzes with cold grays. The posters were in either German or French, and though I had no idea what they were shouting with their bold typefaces and reds and blacks… I knew they were shouting. I would spend hours with these books. I didn't realize it then, but as I sat among Paul's stacks poring over those volumes of nationalist propaganda, I was studying graphic design. I was understanding and responding to a visual language that clearly transcended literal meaning. In short, I had found my life's work.

Still, it took me until I was out of my twenties before I was to land on grateful knees in the world of professional graphic design. I had spent my youth trying with little success to write hit songs in a series of increasingly dysfunctional rock bands and knew a blessing when I saw one. And after I tuned in, the memories of the poster books resurfaced, and with them, I remembered how their designers spoke to a people's pride and their need for answers in a most unstable time through nothing more than a typeface, an image, and a simple color scheme. How they made the invisible emotions and themes visible. A line, a color, an image… These are the disparate elements that I, too, use to transcend literal meaning, to communicate, to make the invisible visible.

BUT THAT'S ONLY PART OF IT, AND SO BEGINS THE JOURNEY INTO MAKING THE INVISIBLE VISIBLE.

THE CLIENT As designers, we don't work in vacuums. We're not fine artists, with only our genius to answer to. We generally have the needs of someone else, often a huge corporation, to consider. Often the most invisible aspect of any design job is your client's desires. I have heard often from New Media designers that their clients "don't know what they want." In my experience that is never the case. It is simply not possible. Part of the process of making the invisible visible is pulling that often seemingly invisible desire out of the space between what the client says and what we hear. And to do that we need to pay attention.

FORM FOLLOWS FUNCTION This Bauhaus maxim rings as true for New Media designers as it did for the German school of architecture and design that coined it in the 1920s. Functionality is another of design's most invisible yet most crucial aspects. The way a site loads is just as important as what loads. Even the most brilliant Flash spot can be rendered worthless if it takes too long to load, streams badly, or crashes a computer.

As New Media designers, then, we have the opportunity to communicate both literal and thematic messages through the double and equal barrels of visual design and functionality/usability.

INSPIRATION Finally, MTIV relates directly to my section on inspiration. There are numerous books published every year with techniques on generating ideas. I have purchased a few... they didn't work. In my experience you don't generate ideas — you beg, borrow, and steal them. Sounds cynical. It isn't. Ideas and inspiration can seem fleeting and frustratingly out of reach — often when you need them most. By developing the ability to see inspiration everywhere and to use that inspiration, regardless of its source, to influence your own work, you make yet another "invisible" — idea/inspiration — visible.

THE THREE SECTIONS OF THIS BOOK I want this book to communicate. I want to clearly lay out the main points of graphic design, as I see them, and have you walk away with something. So I've divided the book into three sections. Like a good design, each part will serve a distinct function that will, in combination with the others, create a whole. Beginning with the basics of how we operate at hillmancurtis, inc. and ending with tips on how to become a better designer, this book is as much a textbook on design as it is an homage to the craft, an exploration of ideas, and an autobiography of myself as an artist in the 21st century.

PROCESS I believe that my company, hillmancurtis, inc., has developed a process that is unique in its ability to help us quickly concept and design consistent and focused New Media... it is that process that I want to share. At hillmancurtis, inc., each project we take on undergoes a unique seven-step process that my staff and I have developed together. It's the process that earned our small shop the honor of redesigning Adobe's Web site, designing its new Studio site, and helping with the design of RollingStone.com. It's the process we've used on a handful of other sites, including a redesign of our own, dozens of Flash motion spots, and finally to conceive, direct, light, and shoot several broadcast and streaming video spots... all in one year.

Some theoretical and some practical, each step is an integral part of the final product. In this section, I'll explain our process in detail and how it allows us to both devise concepts and then generate appropriate design styles quickly to support them.

INSPIRATION To me, inspiration is more than that quick burst of feeling that motivates a creative act. It's the sum of all things that came before you that inform your creative mind. It's every book that's ever moved you, every note that's ever risen above a tune to make you rejoice, every painting you've ever loved. Rarely is it the product of divine epiphany, although I don't discount such instances. Writers and artists have always borrowed from their predecessors. Inspired by African masks, Picasso pioneered what would become cubism in his 1907 painting of a brothel, *Les Demoiselles d'Avignon.* William S. Burroughs applied the montage style of painting to writing in *Naked Lunch* (Grove Press). Young artists in the Renaissance used to learn by apprenticing themselves to their elders, imitating their work. As graphic designers, we're part of this continuum, this history of art and expression. Tapping into that history is embracing inspiration. Our tools may be new, but what we do is as old as cave painting.

This section is a kind of catalog of those who inspire me. Filmmakers, poets, painters, and others who have had a hand in what I do. I'm indebted to them for their contributions to both the art world and, indirectly, to my own work. I include them here so that you may benefit from their words, ideas, and brilliance as I have. And also to help you identify those voices that inspire you.

PRACTICE Finally, this section is aimed at designers like me. Self-taught and hungry for new knowledge. This is a field full of people who have reinvented themselves. People who cannot believe their good fortune at having found something that allows them to be creative, make mistakes, learn from them, pick it up as they go, and help shape one of the most important disciplines of our time. This section is also aimed at those who feel ill-equipped to be designers. Those who think that their expertise in history, literature, or science has no relevance to design. Those who feel ignorant of the programs and confused by the jargon. Phrases such as *kerning*, *Progressive QuickTime*, *legal whites*, *title safe*, *CSS*, *data rate*, *codecs*, and *leading* can leave you spinning if you don't know what they mean. Once a beginner myself, I'll break down the practice of design into a sort of "Everything I ever wanted to know about New Media design basics but was afraid to ask" section.

WHY I WROTE THIS BOOK I have a really varied background. I studied creative writing and film theory in school. Dropped out to tour the UK in a rock band... hitched across America alone after reading *On the Road* by Kerouac (paperback edition from Penguin USA)... and worked every job you can imagine, from dishwasher to housepainter to waiter to nightclub bartender to warehouse worker... so from studying writing and film I gained the ability to recognize themes, but from the horrible jobs I gained this ability to recognize a blessing when I see one... and being a designer is, for me, a blessing. So I honor and respect it and think about it all of the time. I think about ways to improve how I design, how I concept, and how I can more efficiently communicate those invisible themes. What I want to accomplish with this book is this: I want to share our proven process, and I want to impart the respect and excitement I feel for New Media design. Also I want to pack it full of inspirational images... I want it to be a book that designers open while blocked, while looking for ideas, or while questioning their worth as New Media designers. In other words I want to write a book for myself... hopeful that I'm not alone.

PROCESS

MTIV: PROCESS So I'm sitting in this conference room. It's one of those *Dr. Strangelove* rooms you find in modern glass buildings… way down in the guts, through the mazes of cubicles, all pumped air and fluorescent lights. And I'm surrounded by the enemy: two soulless corporate execs and the creative services team that does their bidding. I've just presented my comps for a motion graphic advertisement, and I'm sitting back sipping hazelnut-flavored coffee, thinking to myself, "Why do they try to flavor coffee? It's already got a flavor." Just then, one of the execs leans forward to speak. It's kind of strange how much power a slight lean can have in the hands of the right person. The room quickly falls quiet and all eyes turn….

"What are we trying to communicate here?" the exec asks. Silence. "Hillman, I love the look of these designs, but I don't know if they support our message." More silence.

I was eventually able to speak up and, with help from the members of the creative team, made it through the meeting. Later, back at my office, which at the time was a rented desk in someone else's office, I thought about what had happened. I realized that I had made two key mistakes. I had not presented a design based on a strong theme or concept, and I had identified my clients as the "enemy" to creativity and not as allies in the work of clear, cogent communication. Not wanting to repeat these mistakes anytime soon, I came up with a systematic list of solutions to those problems — a process we follow to this day to concept, develop, and design New Media.

The process consists of seven steps: **LISTEN, UNITE, THEME, CONCEPT, EAT THE AUDIENCE, FILTER,** and **JUSTIFY.**

WORKING WITH THE STEPS The seven-step process we've developed at hillmancurtis, inc. is the result of years spent refining our approach. It started with just a few steps; as it grew, we didn't so much change our methods as hone in and define other steps that, until then, had been intuitive.

From identifying the themes that make up the backbone of an organization and what it's trying to express, to creating a design to support those themes, to filtering out any unnecessary elements, this process guides each of our projects from start to finish.

But this isn't to say it's entirely systematic. While we address each of the seven points in developing any project, we acknowledge their blurred boundaries. Steps often mix, overlap, become one, and work together. Sometimes we need to revisit an earlier step to improve the results of a later one. There are no hard rules, just a willingness to focus on the importance of all seven aspects of the process. Remaining open to change and the bleeding together of ideas is what informs our judgment as artists and creative thinkers.

Thus each chapter in this section will focus on one of the steps, while touching on others in the process. For example, listening must, by definition, involve targeting the theme. Learning how to filter your ideas so that no line is wasted, no bit of memory squandered, and no time lost is intrinsically linked to justifying the end result.

Feel free to jump around, read the chapters out of order, find what interests you, and let that be your guide. I believe in the circular nature of cognition. Parts refer to one another, creating a whole from disparity. Thus a good design, as well as understanding the steps toward accomplishing it, can be digested nonlinearly.

LISTEN Every time I go to San Francisco, whether it's for a conference or a client meeting, I always stay at a certain hotel. The rooms are great and every day at 5:30 they open up the lobby, fill a table with Anchor Steam beer and bottles of California wine…. And the best part is that there's usually a tarot card reader set up in the corner. For ten bucks you can get a reading, and I always do. I've never been that into psychics, readers, and so on, but I tried it once… and I was hooked. Here's why.

She said, "Look. You know what these cards mean. You know what they symbolize. And now I'm going to show them all to you… take a moment and look them over." With that, she spread them all out in front of me, face up. As she did this, I stared at the images and she talked about the huge portion of the brain that scientists have never been able to define. "No one knows what goes on in there," she said, adding her theory that it's in that undefined portion where the subconscious and intuition reside.

She then gathered the cards and stacked them. Then she had me cut the deck, and again, and a third time while she talked about the timeless symbolism of tarot cards, and how their images have spoken to people for thousands of years. Basically, she was saying that I knew intuitively what each card meant, that I could understand this visual language, and that I would remember subconsciously where each card was in the deck, and could thus control the reading. She knew I'd pick the cards I wanted to see.

I could guide her toward the right cards, working with her to bring what I already knew, or at least felt, to the surface. Naturally, once she began reading my fortune, I was rapt, nodding emphatically. She was right on.

As I sat there I became aware of the similarities between what she does and what I, as a New Media designer, do. We both act as interpreters… both using visual language as our tool for revealing. Think about it. The reader basically told me what I already knew. She worked with me to translate my feelings using the cards and her ability to position the cards in an order that started to reveal a bigger, more complete picture. What I do is the same. I meet with a client and listen. I assume that the client knows exactly what he or she wants, and by asking questions and listening, I can help bring those desires to the surface.

A common mistake of designers is thinking of themselves only as visual communicators. We're fortunate to speak the visual language fluently, but we also need to translate literal and thematic messages. In other words, we need to be bilingual. By laying out my cards in a way that revealed a complete picture, the reader helped me translate my feelings into working knowledge. As a designer, I need to listen and ask questions. Those are my "cards," and without them, I'm as good as blind.

WHAT'S MY MOTIVATION? Konstantin Stanislavski, the famous Russian acting teacher, always told his students that no matter what role they're playing, they have to know what their character wants. Everything is driven by desire. In a conversation, both you and the person you're speaking with want something. Always. When meeting with a client, you need to ask yourself not only what they want, but what you want. And in my experience, it's almost always the same thing. I want to understand what they believe, what makes them unique, spotlight their uniqueness, and cast a shadow on their competition. I want to hear a compelling story, uncover the theme that powers that story, and be sold on it. They want to tell me these things and have me help them identify things that are more hidden or abstract. They want to be part of the creative process and have their ideas heard.

And if you believe, as I do, that Stanislavski was right in teaching that everything is driven by desire, then you can use this theory to help craft appropriate questions to ask the client. I often prepare for a client meeting by asking myself exactly what the client's brand or product desires. Because, if you acknowledge that every interaction, whether verbal or visual, is at its core driven by desire, then it makes perfect sense to use this as a tool.

In tuning in like this, you drown out the noise that often thickens the air in a client's office; and what was distorted corporate nonsense becomes the clearly expressed ideas of a collaborator. After all, no one knows a product or brand better than those who spend their days devoted to its promotion.

SWALLOW YOUR PRIDE, OR WHAT IF I ASK A STUPID QUESTION? First off, there are no stupid questions. Prior to the meeting, do as much research as you can on your client and try to form an opinion about their core value or theme. You might be wrong, but at least you have a platform from which to begin asking questions. A good way to start is by placing yourself in the shoes of your client's target customer; you need to involve yourself with the product personally.

Recently, a large financial firm hired us to design a Flash mailer about a fund it had created to be sent out via email to its customers. I'm a designer, not a financier. When these folks were pounding out MBAs at Ivy League schools, I was playing in rock bands… designing posters on the side. But there I was, surrounded by seven or eight people talking about market caps, the S&P, quantitative approach, and so on. As I sat there, trying to make sense out of this whirlwind of business-speak, I realized they were waiting for me to chime in. They wanted to hear my ideas… right then.

I had done some research on the fund prior to the meeting, but nowhere near enough to allow me to keep up with these experts. But I made a decision on the spot. I decided that my job was to try to identify the theme of the fund… the basic value they wanted to communicate to their customers. The financial concepts and terms that had dominated the meeting thus far confused me and would probably have a similar effect on their customers.

So I began to ask a series in an attempt to get a feeling of the fund. The questions were less concerned with the S&P 500 than with why this fund was unique. I asked why the fund was named as it was, how long it had been in existence, and who were the managers and why should I trust them. I placed myself in the shoes of a customer. Someone who had a sum of money and was looking to invest, but had a justifiable fear of the volatile stock market. A customer whose desire or motivation was to be reassured. It worked.

To my surprise my rudimentary questions were greeted enthusiastically and answered patiently. While I gathered pieces of information to use in the design, I also learned the basics of the fund. For them, my questions gave way to an animated, vibrant discussion about their company and what they wanted to communicate. They started talking faster and with more excitement, picking up where the other left off, finishing each other's sentences. And as they bantered ideas about, I began to peel back the layers, revealing to myself the conceptual themes embedded deep inside the numbers talk, the S&P talk, the large cap talk, etc.

My approach to the meeting accomplished two things. Primarily, it helped me understand the fund and its central themes. Secondly, it gave me valuable insight into how my client operated. If they'd grown impatient or annoyed with my basic questions, I'd have pulled out of the job. Without their guidance, I would have been lost.

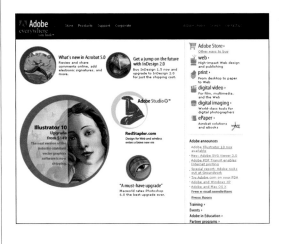

Adobe
everywhere
you look™

Store   Products   Support   Corporate   Adobe Studio | Search | Contact us

 What's new in Acrobat 5.0
Review and share
comments online, add
electronic signatures, and
more.

 **Get a jump on the future
with InDesign 2.0**
Buy InDesign 1.5 now and
upgrade to InDesign 2.0
for just the shipping cost.

 Adobe Store ›
Other ways to buy

 web ›
High-impact Web design
and publishing

 print ›
From desktop to paper
to Web

digital video ›
For film, multimedia,
and the Web

 **digital imaging ›**
World-class tools for
digital photographers

ePaper ›
Acrobat solutions
and eBooks

 **Illustrator 10**
Upgrade
from $149
The next version of the
industry-standard
vector graphics
software is now
shipping.

Adobe Studio ✿™

RedStapler.com
Design for Web and wireless
enters a brave new era

 "A must-have upgrade"
Macworld rates Photoshop
6.0 the best upgrade ever.

Adobe announces

· Adobe Illustrator 10 now
  available
· New: Adobe SVG Viewer 3.0
· Adobe PDF Transit enables
  Internet printing
· Special report: Adobe rocks
  out at Groundwork
· Try Adobe.com on your PDA
· Adobe and Windows XP
· Adobe and Mac OS X
  Free e-mail newsletters

  Press Room

Training ›
Events ›
Adobe in Education ›
Partner programs ›

WHAT'S THE STORY? This is often the best thing to ask first. If I'd known this sitting in that *Dr. Strangelove* conference room, I'd have saved myself the embarrassment of having no response when my client hit me with, "What are we trying to communicate here?"

Had I asked him about the story behind his product, he'd have probed more deeply, giving rise to more questions, and together we'd have begun a dialogue like that with the financial execs discussing their fund. What's more, I'd have learned immediately how to proceed with the design so that it would support his message.

What is the story? Every job has one. A good example of the use of this question working is the Adobe.com site. When we began our redesign of Adobe's Web site during the summer of 2000, I asked flat out: "What's the Adobe story?" — and I got it. I was told how the company started in 1982 with PostScript and then in 1987 unveiled a layout tool called Illustrator, which helped define the desktop revolution. I learned that they have grown and changed with the times. I was told that they have been a step behind, perhaps, in developing applications for the Web, but are catching up and in some cases taking the lead quickly.

I learned about their reputation for producing creative, deeply intuitive design software, digital imaging, and professional authoring tools. They talked about Acrobat, the company's huge contribution to the "e-Paper" market. In fact, people looking for the Acrobat plug-in and application account for a substantial percentage of their site traffic. I listened as my clients explained how each of Adobe's products work together, sharing a common interface, and thus building a solid base of loyal customers. After you learn how to use one application, they said, it's easy to pick up another.

So there it is. One question — What's the story? — and I had the company's history, its points of pride, its shortcomings, and its core values under my belt. And as any designer knows, that much information is pure gold.

LOVE/HATE After finding the story, I like to follow up with a good old-fashioned dichotomy. Have the client look at their current campaign through a black-and-white lens, targeting what they love and hate about it. This, of course, assumes that they have a past upon which you can draw. Nonetheless, it provides a wonderful opportunity to learn from the past and, hopefully, make improvements. You're getting rid of the approaches they were unhappy with, while not erasing elements they were happy with.

To use the Adobe.com site redesign as an example, once again, our account executive on the project, Brigham Field, asked, "What do you hate about the current site?" The room fell silent. People were obviously a little put off — at first. But before long, they were abuzz with discussion. They hated its rigidity, they said — how it was all divided up in squares. They believed the grid layout denied the possibility of presenting more than four features at once. They were unhappy with the global navigation system (GNS), which broke the first rule of GNS: It changed from page to page. The performance of the site was lacking as well; the home page in particular was heavy and slow to load. Finally, they were unhappy with the way the previous design company had interacted with their creative team. They complained about being dictated to and having the final design handed to them with very little attention paid to the talents and ideas of the individuals on their team.

Brigham then asked what they loved about it. Again, silence for a second, then a shift in mood as each person praised different aspects of the site. They liked its graphic qualities, they said, and how it showcased their customers' work. And they liked how it could display the various solutions that Adobe's software provides.

Having asked those two questions, we left the meeting with crucial information that would guide our redesign of their site. And because of our success that day, as well as with the final product, I now include those questions in most of my initial consultations.

TELL THAT TO MY CHEESE CLIENT! I once gave a talk in Philadelphia. I remember it as a wonderful experience, because not only was the audience very gracious and receptive, but after the presentation a few of my key points were directly challenged.

I spoke about listening and finding the theme, then designing everything to support that theme. These points were greeted enthusiastically.

But afterward, as I stood among the attendees, a man approached me, looking most urgent. He stood close and, angling his head toward mine, whispered, "You talk a lot about themes, finding themes, and designing around them, yes?" I took a small, hopefully unnoticed step back and nodded. Again, he leaned forward, looked me in the eye, and said, "Well, tell that to my cheese client."

Looking around, I realized my host was nowhere to be seen, and I knew I was stuck. I tried to answer his question but have no recollection of what I said. Whatever it was, it must not have been convincing because he walked away looking no more satisfied than before we spoke. I was humbled and perplexed. Up to that point, I'd been so impressed with my process that I failed to consider that it might not work for everyone.

On the train ride back to NYC I replayed the conversation over and over, trying to come up with better answers. Right as the train was passing my favorite neon sign… the famous "Trenton makes, the world takes," I accepted the fact that talking about themes in certain meetings would be difficult… but that staying focused on finding the theme would not. In other words, the cheese client might not want to hear some curly-haired bespectacled designer (me) talk to him about the theme of his cheese. In fact he would probably throw me out of his office… but, I guarantee he'll want it communicated in his ads. As the LA designer Steve Kazanjian, founder of the studio *Belief*, perfectly stated, "You have to sell the product, otherwise the design is crap."

You sell the product by spotlighting what is unique about it while casting a shadow on its competitors. Which brings us back to finding out what is unique about the product… its story! What do you want the potential customers to feel as they look at the print ad of the cheese company? Is it that this is the cheapest cheese out there, the best tasting, the best quality? Is it a company that has a history or tradition? You have to know this in order to develop an effective design. Once you've figured out why the cheese is on the market in the first place, you can pinpoint how to sell it. So, dear fellow designer in Philadelphia, this is my answer: Everything, even cheese, has a story; sometimes it's just a little harder to locate.

IN SUM Listening is an activity. It's a matter of asking the right questions in just the right way and then fine-tuning your reception to the answer, however buried it may be. Naturally, different clients need to be treated differently, so it's up to you to determine what the right questions are. Salespeople at high-end boutiques learn to size up customers immediately when they enter the store, allowing the clerks to tap into what they want, thus guiding the sale. Similarly, we need to pay attention to our clients' histories, their ways of communicating, and their needs in order to earn their confidence. Some questions may be inappropriate with certain clients, while other times a simple rephrasing will do. The key is never to alienate them. Think of yourself as their tarot card reader, gently coaxing them towards their fortune, helping them uncover what they want most. You really do have that kind of power.

UNITE I recently met with an old friend who was into his seventh month of marriage. As anyone who's ever been married knows, the first year can be tough, with the sudden adjustments and the discovery of each other's less romantic qualities. While my first year was wonderful, it was also very challenging, so I could relate to what he was going through. He told me that months earlier, when they were practically still newlyweds, he and his wife started having real trouble. They argued frequently, often about the same things time and again. Neither of them understood what was wrong, he told me, and they were wearing thin. Eventually, his wife recommended a couples' counselor, which terrified my friend at first. But after a few sessions, it proved to be the best thing for them.

The counselor worked hard, he said, to create a safe-zone for open expression, giving both of them positive feedback and encouragement as they talked about whatever was bothering them. The success of their relationship, the counselor explained, relied on each person's input and involvement with the program.

In one exercise, they took turns telling the other their complaints, without interruption. Then, the listener was to repeat what they'd heard. As my friend told me about these sessions, he grew more and more excited, clearly thrilled with their results. He said that when they aired their complaints, the very same complaints they'd gone over countless times before, in a controlled environment where the goals from the start were resolution and understanding, they landed more softly and felt less defensive.

They realized that during previous arguments, they weren't really listening to one another. They were listening only long enough to think of a counter to the other's argument. The situation they'd created was adversarial, in which insecurities went unacknowledged. One in which each person felt they weren't being respected, heard, or even included in the argument.

Nineteenth century German philosopher Georg Hegel wrote about arguments as the pursuit of a greater truth reached by, yet transcending both sides. Using the term "dialectic," he described the process as one of points and counterpoints, or theses and antitheses, which ultimately lead to a synthesis. Thus an argument can be seen less as a conflict and more as an evolution. In other words, by listening to and acknowledging the other's viewpoint, even the hottest argument can end gracefully.

Through the sessions, my friend and his wife learned not only how to communicate with one another but also that equal communication would be crucial to the success of their marriage.

It was during this conversation that I realized I'd found the perfect way to introduce this step of our process at hillmancurtis. Like a marriage, the success of any project relies on each member of the creative team. And by "creative team," I mean everyone involved, from the client to the designers.

"We're all making the same movie," wrote Sidney Lumet, the great American filmmaker (*Dog Day Afternoon, Serpico, The Morning After*), in his 1995 book, *Making Movies* (Vintage Books), on the importance of acknowledging every producer, actor, production assistant, and caterer who works on his films. Whatever their individual role is, he stressed, everyone is united by a singular goal: to make the same movie.

And though they're all making a film, it's still the filmmaker who leads the way. As a designer, it's your responsibility to orchestrate that unity for a design project; you need to join the hands of the account execs with the project managers, your codesigners with the clients… ensuring that everyone feels both important and included in the process.

INCLUSION I start each project with the assumption that everyone involved is creative. I really believe this. While some people's creativity may not be readily apparent, it's there and not to be disregarded. So whenever appropriate, I kick off the first meeting by telling everyone in the room, at the conference table, or on the phone that I believe in their creativity and that I intend to utilize it. In other words, I make it clear that I can't produce a great design without them. I make it clear that we share responsibility for the final product, and more often than not, they accept that responsibility with pleasure.

And this isn't just PR hype. Remaining open to the client's feedback is just as important back at the design office. I try to encourage openness to change and a general sense of respect among my staff so that a client's suggestions are never dismissed outright or greeted with frustration. I remind them that the design is, first and foremost, about the client's message. It's a delicate balance between identifying with the design personally and allowing enough room for it to develop through the input of others. Regardless of how uncreative they may seem.

The more corporate the setting, the easier it is to think of yourself as the only creative type in the room. I often find myself surrounded by such starched-shirts that my messy hair, dopey glasses, and bad posture make me feel like a headbanger in a monastery. But as soon as I open the gates by asking for their ideas, and really wanting to hear them, the superficial differences that often obstruct the flow of creativity dissolve away, leaving just people with a singular goal: to make the same design.

Still, there will be times when you'll need to tap into your client's creativity more covertly. With particularly touchy or formal clients, I'll simply ask, "What do you think?" This helps me include them in the process with one simple question. The point is that they're involved in generating ideas and directing the project, if only through vetoing what you suggest.

INVOLVE THE CLIENT EARLY AND OFTEN No one likes to be kept in the dark, especially when money is at stake. Your clients aren't just trusting you to communicate their message; hopefully they're paying you too. If you have a few meetings and then disappear, only to resurface a week later with a near-finished design, you'll most likely have a pretty unhappy client on your hands. So I always include a healthy amount of time dedicated to client feedback in the time estimates we submit with our proposals. That way I make it clear from the start that we intend to involve them in every step of the process.

There's a fear that including a client in every step of the process will lead to micromanaging and that they'll drive you crazy with uncalled-for creative direction. In some cases, the fear is justified. But more often, I've found it to work the other way. It's like any relationship: The more respected a client feels, the more secure he'll feel with your work and the less he will feel the need to watch your every move, thus giving you more freedom as a designer. The dialogue you establish through regular updates also allows the design to grow organically through a mixing of your ideas with their's, you and your client taking turns guiding the other toward the best design possible. It's funny, but it's when I'm most convinced that a client is wrong that the project grows the most. The feedback spurs debate, which sets us off on a dialectic that ends in a synthesis of creative thought.

Feedback also helps us avoid costly pitfalls such as slaving away on an idea that we think is the coolest, only to submit it to a client who doesn't like it — or worse, doesn't "get it." And the longer you work on anything, the more emotionally attached you become, making it harder to understand another's point of view.

ESTABLISH GOALS EARLY Graphic design is not fine art… it's not something that you do alone in a loft… You have partners whether you like it or not. Those partners can be your client, your coworkers, the project manager, or the account exec. I always try to treat them like partners who can help guide the project toward success and not as hindrances to my creativity. So by its nature, graphic design/New Media design is a collaborative craft, which is wonderful because it presents so many opportunities to learn.

But like any partnership, collaboration can sometimes be difficult. I have found that when I am clear from the start with my concept and direction and, most importantly, the project goal, it's easier. In other words, if you include the client in your early thoughts as to appropriate concepts and possible themes and are clear with them that the goal is to communicate a message… usually a single message… working together is easier.

Problems arise when either the clients or the designers feel insecure, and the insecurities are often the same on both sides. "Will my clients like it?" wonders the designer, while for the clients, it may be, "Will my boss like it?" As a designer, you might feel compelled to throw in a lot of "wow" design elements… bells and whistles that will "blow them away." Likewise, the clients may want you to include every marketing slogan, every feature of the product, or every aspect of the brand in an effort to cover their backs. But both are examples of insecurities getting in the way of communication. Unjustified elements merely widen the gulf between the viewer and the message.

Recognizing these insecurities at the beginning is the best way to solve them. It allows you to stay consistent throughout the project and prevents either you or your client from feeling lost.

There's also a series of smaller steps that we set to help us establish and share the goal of the project early.

First, we always draft a creative brief. It doesn't need to be a twenty-page document, but it does need to clearly establish the project goal and point out the creative steps we'll take to reach it. Next comes a story board or site map. In the case of motion work, storyboards are quite literal, mapping out the linear progression of the project. For Web sites, the maps allow us to interact with the client, making sure that the site functions properly and is clear and consistent in its navigation. The point is to create documents — creative briefs, storyboards, and site maps — that your team can share to establish the goal of the project prior to actually jumping into the design.

So in addition to the ultimate goal, smaller goals may need to be met along the way — and establishing what they are with your client is no less important than agreeing on the final product.

REMEMBER YOUR GOALS The worst thing for a creative team is a project that isn't working. We recently designed a Web site for a nonprofit in California for considerably less than our standard fee. But we believed in the nonprofit's cause and wanted to be part of it.

It was a tough job because the client was initially having trouble returning consistent feedback. And without the client's guidance we took a couple of wrong turns in our design. Somewhere in the back of our minds also lurked the fact that we were doing the job below our usual fee and it became tempting to cut a corner here and there.

The inconsistent feedback from the client pushed the schedule out quite a bit, and we started to grow impatient with the project. Our design team worked in silence and became more and more grumpy, even as the project neared completion. While the client was relatively pleased with our design, we weren't. We knew that on some basic level, it just didn't work. We knew that we weren't implementing a cohesive system but creating a patchwork of half-baked efforts. We knew this because we're designers. For us, it's ultimately not about money or prestige. It's about making something we can be proud of, something that showcases our ability to communicate through design. And we weren't doing our job.

So one morning, I met with the design team to revisit our original goals for the project. Immediately, it became clear that we'd lost sight of those goals. The organization we were designing for produces a product that's easy to use, stable, and reliable, providing security for children in local communities. Our design, however, was inconsistent, clunky, and difficult to navigate. Ultimately, the inconsistencies in design and poor functionality were negative reflections on the product and company as a whole.

So the design team and I sat down at a computer and started identifying the various flaws. We visited and studied other sites we admire and literally made changes on our own in real time as we talked. By the end of the day, we'd developed a stronger, cleaner design that we could believe in. And even though it meant we'd have to start all over, we felt excited and relieved. We knew we'd be happier working overtime than feeling that we'd failed as graphic artists.

The goals of any project can be looked at as a shared philosophy of the team, and if the philosophy of the team is not being honored, the team starts to fall into bad habits.

In this case we lost sight of the goals and failed to communicate them consistently throughout the project… which led to a divided team. We lost our shared philosophy for the job. Fortunately, we were able to remind ourselves in time to make changes.

SELLING THE DESIGN I had an experience recently in which a subcontractor we hired was giving us a review of his first comps. He had prepared a typed presentation that he read from verbatim as he showed us the designs. He read this presentation, explaining why certain elements were here or there, why the font was selected, and how size and scale were used, and I thought to myself… never, never sell your design. You should be able to lay out your comps in front of the clients and if you have heard them, stayed true to their desires, and included them in the creative process, the designs should speak for themselves. The clients should be able to look at the designs and see a bit of themselves. You can stay quiet, answer their questions if necessary, and listen to their feedback… take notes and bring it closer on the next rev. I always tell my designers that if they ever find themselves saying…"and here we have" or "we used the Helvetica font because it's simple, yet strong… blah blah blah" then they haven't done their job. Resist the temptation to sell your designs, because it's not about educating your clients as to how and why design works… they already know! They have been responding to graphic design all their lives.

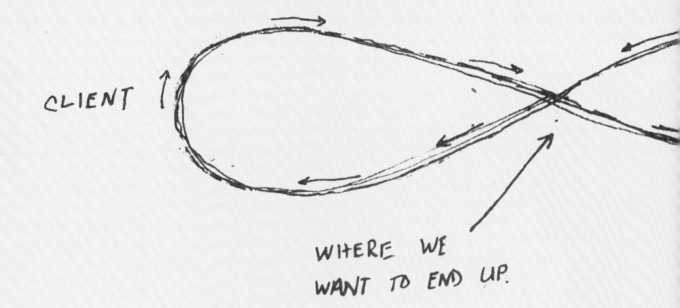

CLIENT

WHERE WE
WANT TO END UP.

IN SUM Cooperation is the foundation of any team effort. It's a basic idea, one that goes all the way back to kindergarten when your teacher pleaded with you to cooperate with others. But as basic as it is, we all forget its importance.

Keeping the channels of communication open between yourself and your client is a craft. It takes practice and work, but its rewards always outweigh the costs. Granted, a marriage is for life, while a design project lasts only a few weeks. But the mentality you develop as a designer and the ability to create a community out of the diverse cast that makes up a given project will last a lifetime. And most of all, when people band together, there's virtually no limit to what can be achieved.

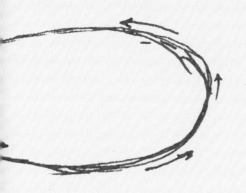

CREATIVE AGENCY

TARGET THE THEME When I was in college, studying creative writing, one of my best friends, Dave Souvlewski, turned me on to *On the Road* by Jack Kerouac (paperback edition from Penguin USA). I read the book in a day and a half… staying up all night. It's a story of two friends, Sal Paradise and Dean Moriarty… loosely based on Mr. Kerouac and his real life friend, Neal Cassady. It follows these two as they devour America. Traveling coast-to-coast in beat-up cars with nowhere to go, but in a hurry to get there. They're beatniks, dropouts, and losers, spitting in the face of conservative 1950s America… way off into black jazz musicians, poetry, going out all night and all day in pursuit of anything and everything. I couldn't believe these guys and their adventures. The book read like an open invitation to a once-in-a-lifetime party.

So we took off. Dave managed to get a bright orange Camaro that needed to be delivered to New Jersey… we were in San Francisco. And so began our adventure. We sped across the country in a few days and split up on the East Coast. Dave started hitching west on his own, and a few days later, after working up my nerve, I found a scrap of cardboard and with a black marker wrote "New Orleans" on it.

Stepping out onto a freeway, I held out the sign and waited.

On the Road is 307 pages long. I can remember parts of it, here and there, but I'll always remember the theme. The theme of the book is reckless discovery. And the book is so effective because it never forgets that theme. Its passages read like a car speeding crazily across a freeway. The prose rambles feverishly, without the restrictions of punctuation. Rather, simple dashes pepper the book with their short pauses, like Charlie Parker taking a breath between phrases. And it's not so much the plot that made me step out on the freeway, cardboard sign in hand… it was the theme.

Themes have that power. They can communicate so much deeper than literal messaging. As designers we have an opportunity to draw attention to theme through our designs. Every product has a theme, every company, every brand. Our challenge as designers is to target a given project's theme and use it as a guide that will influence every design decision we make from the initial concept to the final composition. Without communicating a theme, our designs will simply be pretty pictures… a bouquet of roses with no note attached.

TARGETING At our studio we use a process to "target" themes. It's one thing to identify the theme of a book or a movie — there's usually no great hurry — but with design, especially New Media design, we're often chasing a deadline before even accepting the project. Quickly identifying the theme can make all the difference in a project's success. Because once you know the theme of your design, questions can be answered.

HERE'S WHAT WE DO Before meeting with a client, one of my designers or I actually draw a three-ring target on a piece of paper, leaving a little room in the right margin. Once in the meeting, we start asking questions about the project. As the client talks, we listen (as I described in step one) for words and ideas they repeat and get excited about. One of us then jots down those words in the space beside the target, giving us both a literal list as well as a shared visual workspace where we can begin to identify and work toward the theme of our design.

I've found that just having that piece of paper in front of me makes it easier to ask questions, listen for key words, and chase down incomplete answers with more specific questions. Sometimes, when I'm especially comfortable with the client, I'll even draw the target right in front of them, explaining my process as I do so. I tell them that I want their help in finding the heart of their product or brand, its emotional epicenter, and ask them to give me six or seven words they believe to reflect it. From those six or seven words, we'll work together to determine which one goes in the center of the target, thus becoming our theme and single source of gravity for the project.

An excellent example of this is a project we did for Iomega, a company that makes Zip and Jaz disk drives, both portable storage formats for computer media. Kim Carter, a partner with Iomega's ad agency, Euro RSCG DSW Partners, and Jared Allen, DSW's art director, called me one day to describe what they had in mind. It was right before the turn of the century, late 1999, and the company wanted a Flash spot that would capitalize on the Y2K panic in order to showcase their technology. At the time people were terrified that the Y2K "bug" would crash their computers, permanently erasing their valuable files. With this in mind, I immediately began picturing a scary ad: distressed fonts, frenetic motion, and apocalyptic imagery. I was excited about all the fun I could have with it, thinking of motion designer Kyle Cooper's harrowing film titles for *Seven, Sphere,* and *The Island of Dr. Moreau.*

So I went into the meeting with my paper target, ready to fill up the margin with words like "Horror," "Disaster," and "Crash." But to my surprise, at the end of the meeting, I had these instead: "Safe," "Secure," "Action," "Approaching," "Problem," and "Solution." The closest they came to my original list was "Chaos," but it was lost amongst the positive words that surrounded it.

I went back to my office and studied the list. I began thinking about the company — its history, values, and products — having asked these details about the company in the meeting. After some thought, I realized that the company really does one thing: it designs and manufactures disk drives for the safe backup of computer media. And the company revolves around that one thing all the time, Y2K scare or not. From the words I had, I knew the company's core value wasn't chaos or fear, but security. So in the target's center, I wrote, "Secure"; in the second ring, "Solution"; and in the third, "Problem" and "Approaching." Instead of designing an ominous, reactive spot, I knew we had to design a proactive one — a design that would draw attention to the core thematic value of the company and its products.

With my target and the direction of DSW's creative team, we created a design that both addressed the pressing Y2K concern and revealed the company's overall message — that it provides security, and always has. Granted, the spot starts with the words "Y2K is coming," but replace them with something like "Big project finally finished?" and it still works. Because if the company's core values transcend time and the specific problem, so should its design.

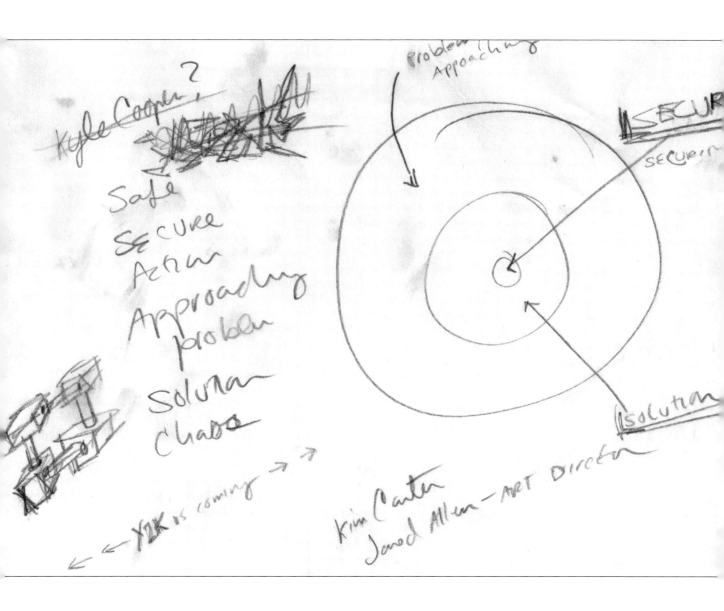

Kyle Cooper ?

Safe
SECURE
Action
Approaching
problem

Solution
Chaos

← ← Y2K is coming → →
←

Problem Thing
Approaching

SECURE
securing

solution

Kim Carter
Jared Allen — Art Director

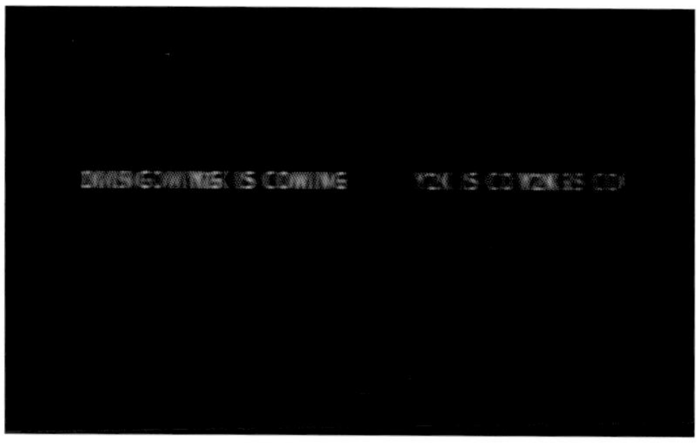

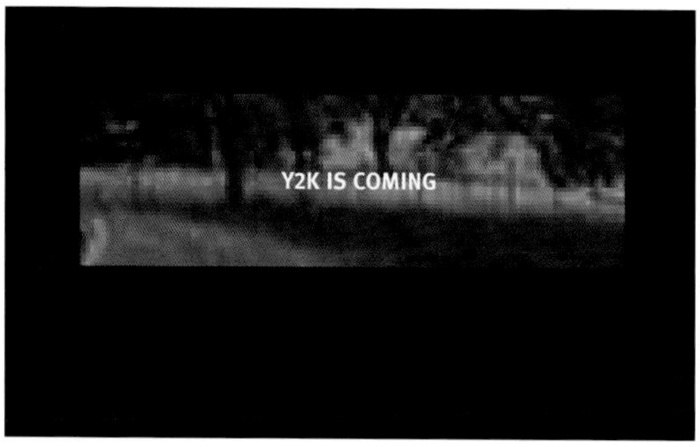

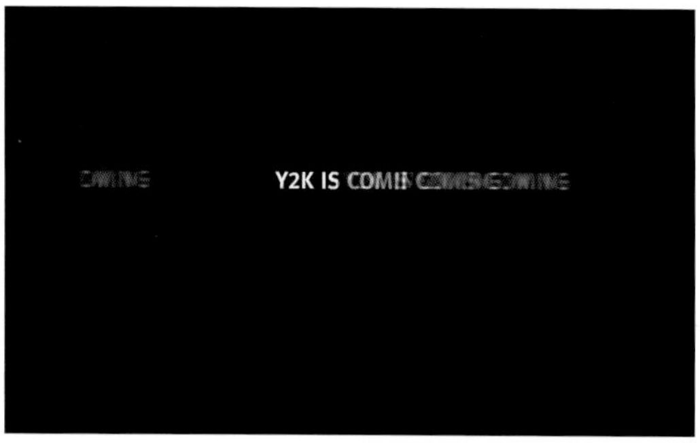

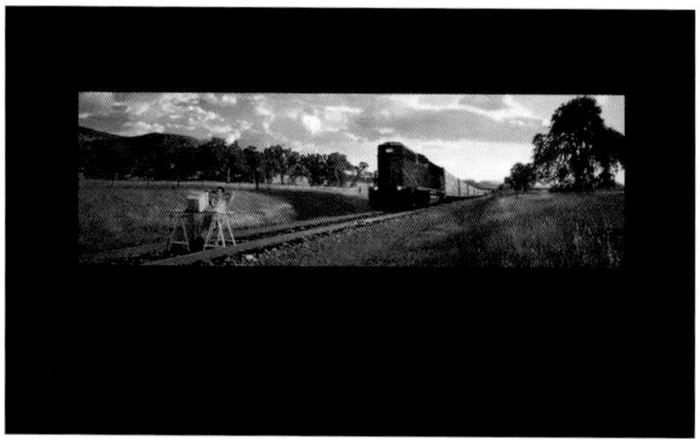

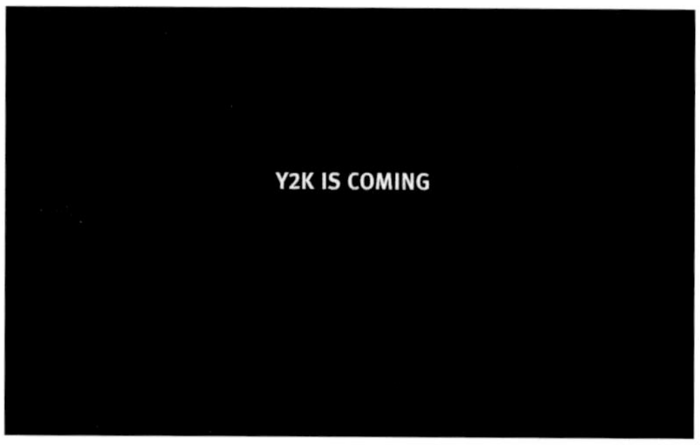

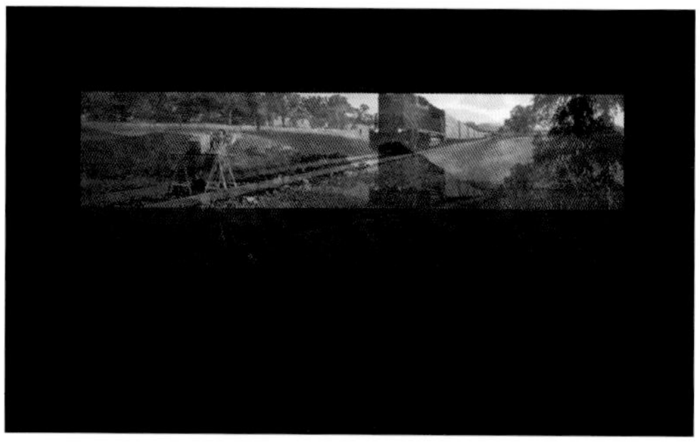

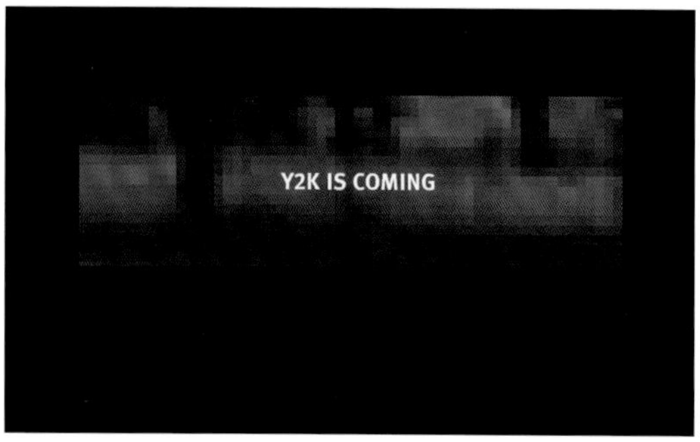

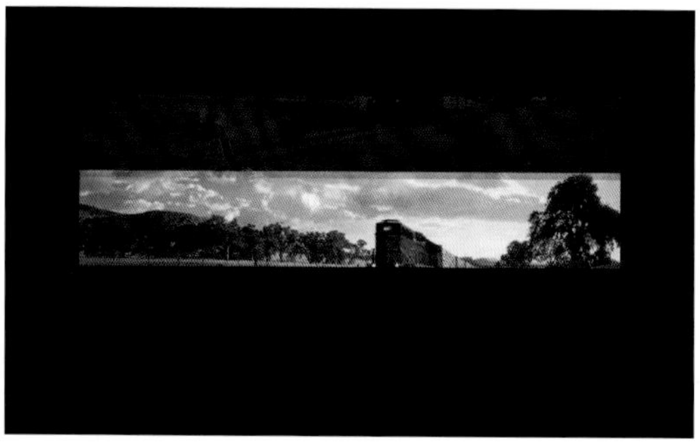

FLASH AD **Client:** Iomega **Ad Agency:** EURO RSCG DSW Partners

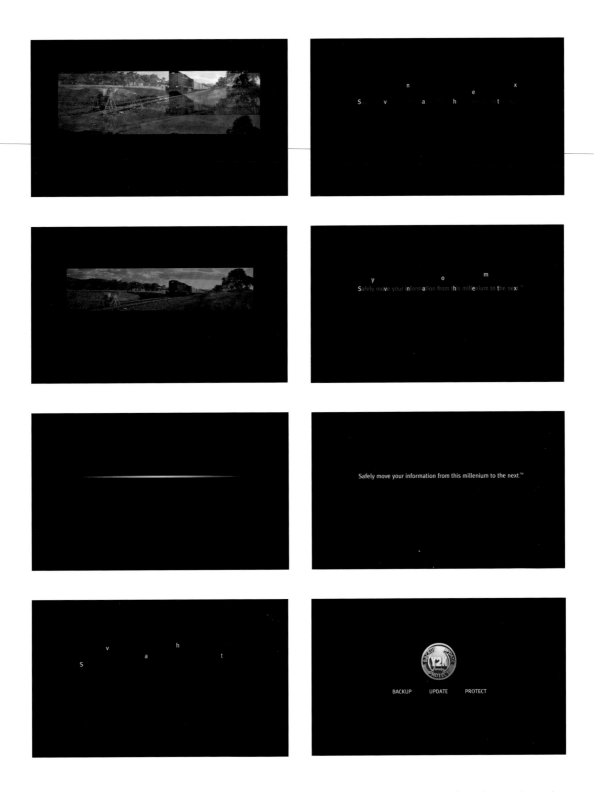

THEME LEADS TO STYLE In the book *Making Movies* (Vintage Books), Sidney Lumet wrote that determining the style of a movie can be described as "… a slow process of investigation where style emerges from a constant reiteration of the theme. Long discussions with the writer, cameraman, production designer, and editor allow the design to, in a sense, present itself."

This is essentially what we are doing with our targets and words. We are discussing the project in hopes that we can identify the theme first, and from that theme allow the style to emerge.

A great example of this working is a site design we did, again, for Adobe: the Adobe Studio site.

I first met with Adobe's creative team in San Francisco during March of 2000 to discuss a new site that would exist in tandem with the main corporate site. Adobe Studio, they said, would be a resource for design professionals; a place where they can get tips and community services, read interviews with designers, and access a robust online project management and file storage application. A pretty tall order, but I got it immediately. Basically, it was to be a site for people like me — one I could visit daily to keep up with the industry, view other designers' work, learn new techniques, find the latest fonts and plug-ins, and manage our current projects.

I hadn't gotten the job yet, but there was great chemistry between us. Recognizing that chemistry, I felt comfortable enough to tear out a piece of paper and sketch the target, explaining to them why as I did it. I then asked everyone from their team to come up with a couple of words that they thought might describe the theme or core purpose of their new destination site.

After a bit of back and forth, I had jotted down "Inspiration," "Community," "Instruction," "Simple," "Creative," "Collaboration," and "Products (Selling, Promoting, and Supporting)." Talking more, we eventually identified "Community" as the central theme for the site. Looking back, it seemed obvious that the site is a place to gather information, learn, get inspired, find tools for your latest job, and communicate with other members of the Adobe design community… but it actually took us a good 45 minutes to agree. So in the center of the target we wrote a big "Community" and, in the outer two rings, "Inspiration" and "Instruction."

Three months later we had finished the site, and every design decision we made was determined by our theme. For example, in our color palette we avoided blacks (too mysterious and claustrophobic), grays, and whites (too cold). Instead, we chose warm tones. We wanted to support "Community" and design a place where a visitor would feel welcome. Warm tones did that. We also stayed away from frenetic or jarring motion on the pages that had LiveMotion animations. Instead we designed motion with elements that built upon each other or had moves that brought elements together… all in a smooth and organic flow. The idea again is to use all of your visuals, including motion, to present a style that supports and draws attention to the theme… in this case a community that welcomes, grows, and brings people together.

WHAT'S THE THEME? An exercise I practice whenever I see a movie, read a short story, or visit an art gallery is to ask myself, "What's the theme?" It's amazing how the more you do this the easier it gets. Finding a theme actually becomes second nature. This is valuable because it carries over to your design work and becomes a natural part of your process.

I recently rented the movie *High Fidelity*. After seeing it once, I decided the central idea behind this old "boy has girl, loses her, and gets her back" story is renewal. John Cusack, the film's central character, is metaphorically frozen, and through the power of love is able to thaw and bloom into a new man. A bit hack, I know, but I'm a sucker for stuff like this.

So I went back and watched it again, paying special attention to the directing, cinematography, lighting, editing, and art direction to see how they support the theme I'd identified. What I noticed was a small touch from the film's art director: the color green appears in small doses throughout the film. The sad story is well placed in cold, industrial Chicago, where muted grays dominate; but green still pervades, if only slightly. Even at a funeral, there's a man wearing a green shirt in the background of the shot.

This subtle touch provides a subconscious string of hope that runs through the movie, revealing a close-knit creative team behind the film's production. It shows that the film's art director was aware of the power color can have to communicate a feeling — hence the green walls in Cusack's apartment, a stack of green record sleeves in his store, and the locale of many of his flashbacks (a city park in spring). The style of the film, with its somber tones offset by the recurring green, reflects its theme of apparent hopelessness giving way to new beginnings.

The art director had made a conscious stylistic decision based on the theme. It's not enough to arbitrarily pick a color... if you have the opportunity to use color, choose one that draws attention to the theme. Green is the color of spring, and spring is the season of renewal.

Another thing I do almost daily, as I mentioned at the start of this book, is watch the trailers on Apple.com/quicktime. These are sixty-second bursts of theme. Yes, they give you an idea of the story, but, ultimately, they draw you in with theme. Try a few... and immediately after watching ask yourself, "What's the theme?" Then watch them again and pay attention to how the style of the editing, lighting, art direction, score, motion graphics, and cinematography support that theme.

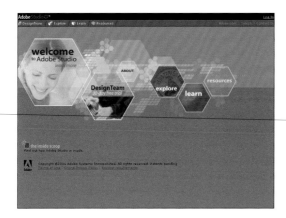

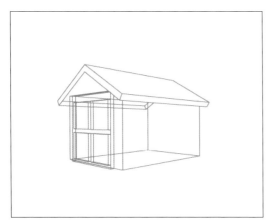

the most complete

radicals

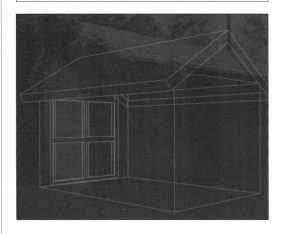

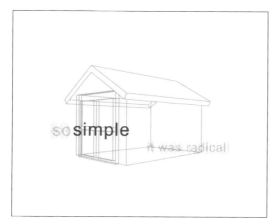

IN SUM There's nothing like a really well-told story. A great book or film reaches millions with the universal relevance of its story. But what makes a story relevant? More often than not, the details bear no similarity to your own life at all. I loved *High Fidelity*, although I don't live in Chicago, I've never owned a record store, and I've been happily married for eight years. But I can relate to the pain of loss and the sense of renewal. Likewise, I may not be an ex-football-star-cum-poet who dropped out of Columbia, but reckless discovery is a theme I know well.

Graphic design also works on multiple levels. Each level is important, because a story needs to be told, but that story is really just a vehicle for the theme. Whether it's a computer bug, a new product, or an old idea, the subject of a story must not only point to something greater than itself but also communicate that idea effectively. And that idea, with its staying power and transcendent message, is the theme.

By employing a process for targeting themes and by getting in the habit of recognizing themes in movies, books, art — really all of the different forms of creative expression — we are able to identify a project's theme more effectively. And through our craft, make that theme visible, supporting it with every design decision we make.

CONCEPT Remember Pink Floyd? In the early 1980s, my friends and I would hang out for hours listening to their hugely popular, epic double-album *The Wall*. One day one of our group's more sophisticated members announced that it was a "concept album." I was lying flat on my back, eyes closed, and I remember nodding in solemn agreement. But in truth, I was clueless. Concept album? To me, the album was a collection of songs, just like any album, some good and some bad.

Shortly thereafter, I finally got it. All those songs are linked together, each one telling a different chapter of the same story. All illustrating a central theme: isolation. Or, more specifically, the building of a psychological wall to keep society away.

I never heard the album the same way again. It became a multifaceted journey, a deep and compelling story around which to wrap my 19-year-old mind. I started to relate to the protagonist — a lonely man lashing around within the confines of his own psyche — and I began to fancy myself likewise complex, and maybe even a little disturbed. Looking back, I can't help but smile. Nevertheless, I related to it so strongly because its theme was so brilliantly executed. Every note, vocal nuance, and lyric plays into what the album is about. And the sum total of those elements is *The Wall's* concept. The album's theme, isolation, is told through the story of a troubled rock star grappling with his past and a crippling sense of alienation. In other words, the story carries the message.

This was my first lesson in conceptual thinking, and it's one I'll never forget because I've come to recognize concepts as one of the trickiest, yet most important aspects of any creative endeavor. Without a solid concept, all you have is a bunch of disparate parts competing for attention instead of collectively forming a whole.

"INFINITY" AD FOR BIC BALLPOINT PENS **Ad Agency:** TBWA\Hunt\Lascaris (South Africa)

A DEFINITION OF SORTS Think of it this way: a concept is an idea. Our job as designers is to visually explain that idea.

Take for example this brilliant ad for BIC ballpoint pens designed by TBWA\Hunt\Lascaris. It's a great concept visually explained — the pen lasts forever. It also implies that the pen is a vehicle to express your ideas forever — so not only does it make a point for the value of the product, but it also attaches positive implications to the BIC brand.

Concept is also a means through which you illustrate your theme. The theme here is "value." The concept supports it wonderfully.

Contagiouspictures.com is a site we produced in the fall of 1999, a Web site for a professional photographer named Nick Kudos. Best known for his PhotoDisc series, Nick was looking to expand his practice to include film and video work. He came up with the title "Contagious Pictures," hoping his short films would be funny enough that they'd generate a viral buzz.

So we began thinking about the idea of contagion, of a virus spreading rampantly from person to person, and we landed on a solid concept: people sneezing on each other. We filmed people from the office sneezing and then used those shots as the site's buttons. Moving the cursor over a person (button) on the site causes them to sneeze not germs, but letters; and those letters spell out Contagious. The site thus communicates the theme behind Nick's business to everyone who visits it.

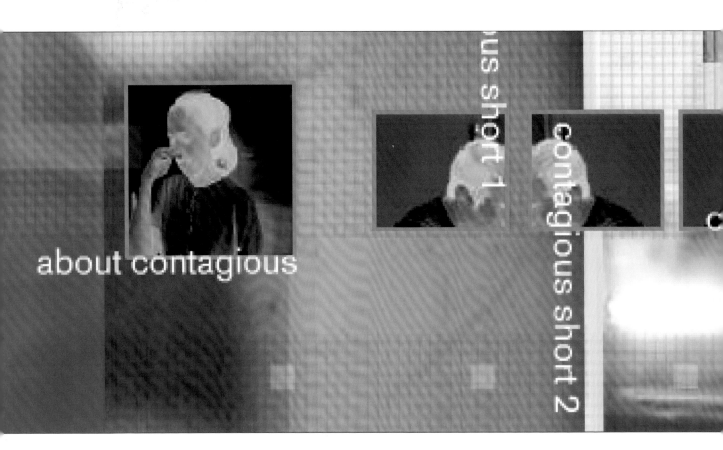

about contagious

contagious short 1

contagious short 2

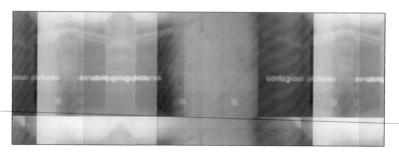

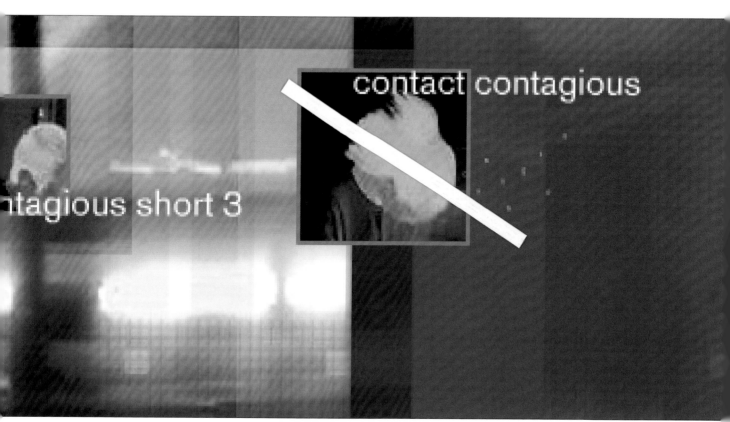

WORKING TOWARD CONCEPT "Suddenly the answer was right in front of me, crystal clear... it came out of nowhere." We've all heard this statement in some form... we've all said it ourselves. It implies that ideas and concepts appear from somewhere unexplained... like epiphanic sparks. And I believe they do... sometimes. More often, though, we have to work toward that wonderful idea. One of the designers at hillmancurtis, inc., Grant Collier, appropriately describes it as a journey. And what he means is that you usually start with a myriad of ideas and possibilities and hack your way through them until you end up face-to-face with something, if you're lucky, as richly conceptual as the BIC ad.

So how do you "work toward" that concept? As with all things creative, there's no single way to do this, but I'll share some of the methods we use in my studio.

SKETCHING I always start conceptualizing the same way. After my initial client meetings and after we've identified the theme, I start to draw. Aside from being a relaxing thing to do, you never know when a basic sketch will grow into a full concept. In fact, many of my best ideas come from sketching, usually because they're the simplest. So I try to spend a few hours sketching for each project I take on.

If it's a motion spot, I'll sketch out a few frames of a possible sequence, or maybe a move or two. All the while, I remain focused on how the motion will communicate the theme, and make my decisions accordingly. Sometimes I'll even doodle my ideas directly on the computer to create a "motion test." Usually about five to ten seconds long, motion tests allow me to gauge how well the idea works and also to post the sample for my client to see.

A while back, 3Com hired us to do a Flash spot for a home digital subscriber line (DSL) hookup they provide called HomeConnect. The company wanted the site to communicate "the simplest way to get fast Internet connections," and I immediately began sketching moves. I wanted to express "fast downloads," so I sketched out ways of making text zoom in on pictures quickly. The sketches led to a rough storyboard, which I presented to the company prior to starting work in Flash. After being completed, our design went beyond a run-of-the-mill marketing campaign by actually embodying the product's function.

If the project is a Web site, I'll sketch out a quick site map. Or if the client has already developed one, I'll redraw it, and think about ways to simplify it. Then I start sketching wireframes, experimenting with the placement of essential elements such as logos, menu options, and other navigational features.

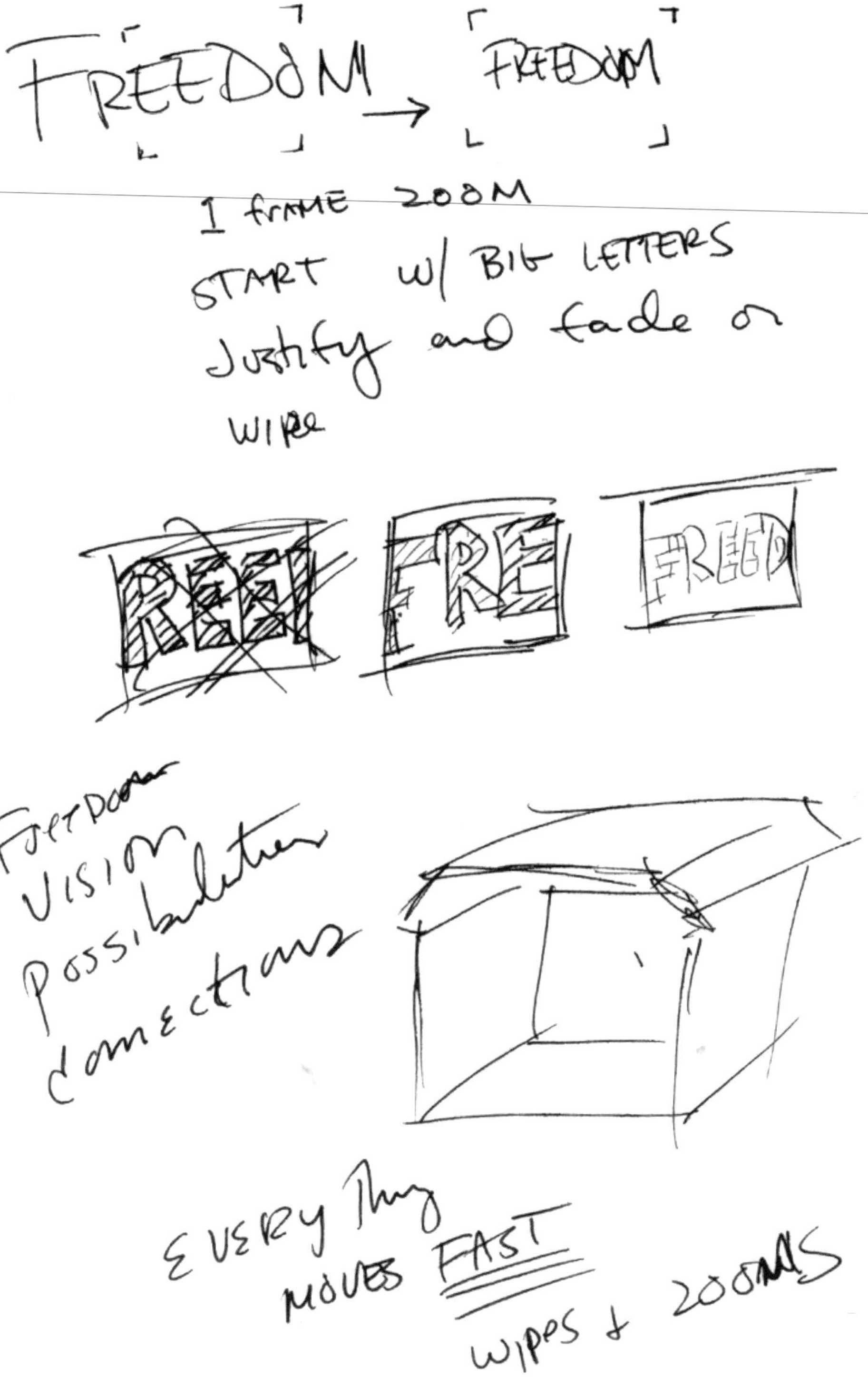

FREEDOM → FREEDOM

I frame ZOOM
START w/ BIG LETTERS
Justify and fade on
WIPe

REEL   FRE   FREED

FREEDOM
VISION
possibilities
connections

EVERY Thing
MOVES FAST
WIPES & ZOOMS

3COM HOMECONNECT FLASH AD   **Client:** 3Com   **Ad Agency:** Foote, Cone & Belding (San Francisco)

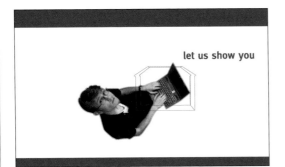

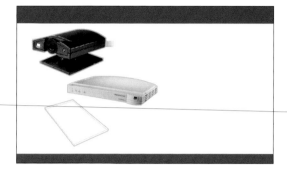

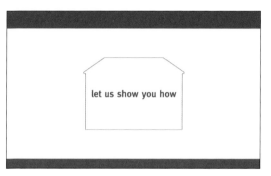

STORYBOARDING After sketching, I start taking stabs at telling the story, from beginning to end, and combining images with text to see what works. The storyboard is basically a formalization of the concept, with which you mentally and visually puzzle out how you'll realize your idea.

Everyone involved in the project needs to be together at this point because you never know which creative collaboration will lead to the perfect sequence. Sometimes it's the copywriter and the art director, sometimes two designers, sometimes the client and your whole staff. Wherever the idea's born, once the juices start to flow, the project really begins to take shape.

Don't let storyboarding intimidate you. It's not nearly as final a step as it may sound. It, too, goes through multiple revisions and false starts before it gels. By the time I send a final storyboard off to a client for approval, I've usually filled up countless scraps of paper and napkins with thumbnail sketches, scrawled away in my sketchbook, and tooled for hours in Adobe Illustrator and Photoshop building a digital version of the board. Remaining freeform is the best way to avoid creative paralysis.

COLLABORATE WITH YOUR CLIENT As I discussed in step one, involving the client is a fundamental part of creating a successful design. They need to like what you come up with, of course, but they can also offer valuable insights into their company that could hugely influence your concept. We went into Cysive, Inc., for example, with a pretty detailed concept already developed — so did the company's project manager, Mike Hayes. Instead of clashing with him, however, we took his ideas back to our office and let them guide our second version. And even though we didn't use his designs directly, they influenced our's through what they told us about Cysive's core values. Our final concept, therefore, was genuinely inspired by his involvement, and the company loved it.

Other times, a client will provide a perfect idea, and maybe even a great storyboard, making your job infinitely easier. We had the honor of working with the illustrator Craig Frazier last spring to create a series of Web and broadcast spots, and our role in the project was primarily that of producer. For each piece in the series, Craig provided a storyboard that clearly communicated his concept in a linear and visual manner, allowing my team to really focus on the technical aspects of its production.

The Craig Frazier animations are an interesting example of the organic nature of our process. Ideally we like to start targeting the theme with a client and then building a concept around that theme. But in this case, we received a detailed storyboard that literally mapped out every step of the animation. We really had no idea of themes that could power these animations, but going over the storyboard a few times, target pages in hand, we quickly identified them. And while the linear sequence was already determined for us, we could use score, pacing, editing effects, and movement to communicate those themes.

Country drive page 1 of 2
5.22.01
Craig Frazier Studio

Open on bird in tree, car coming into frame in background.

Cut to close-up of driver. Background scenery speeds by.

Cut to dramatic view of car driving right to left.

Dissolve to overhead with car moving up the road. Cows silouetted in the far distance.

Cut to silouette of car driving by cows.

Cut to view of driver scanning herd of all black cows.

Car slows as he sees a spotted cow.

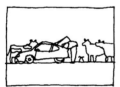

Cut to car stopped in front of spotted cow. Driver digs in his trunk.

Cut to show him walking with pale and milking stool. Cows watch on.

Cut to car pulling away.

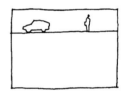

Cut to silouette of car stopping and driver getting out with pale.

Cut to close-in. Figure is blowing white bubbles.

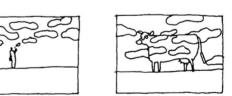

Pull back to reveal more and more bubble-clouds.

Dissolve to spotted cow with clouds passing through and behind him. fade to black.

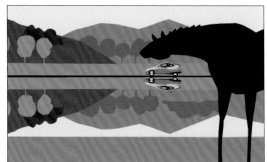

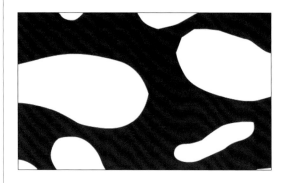

 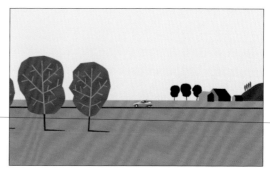

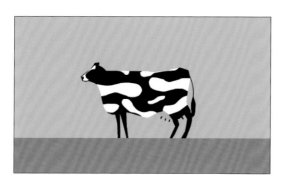 

LET THE MEDIUM HELP Some media are simply more conducive to certain concepts than others. Working with The FeedRoom, for example, we were challenged to reflect the theme of "humanness" — not an easy task. So our creative director, Ian Kovalik, who was in charge of the project, considered several options, and finally hit upon one that actually capitalizes on the Web's limitations. Ian wanted to have two people dance, jump, and walk around the screen, leading the visitor from scene to scene. Realizing from the start that we would use Flash for this job, we first considered shooting videos of real people and animating them as sequential frame-by-frame bitmaps, but their movements would have been choppy and rough — in a word, inhuman. So we decided that vector-based animation was the way to go, and created a Flash spot in which silhouetted figures perform with the grace of real people. And not only do they move beautifully, but the site can be streamed over low-bandwidth Internet connections, making it accessible to the greatest number of people possible. So in this case, respecting the medium and its limitations opened a conceptual door for us and helped make the spot unique.

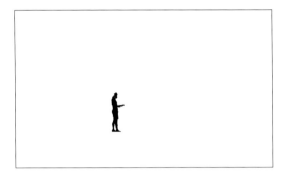

NEVER STOP THINKING Great designs don't come from recipes, and you generally can't predict a final outcome. Uncertainty is a cornerstone of the creative process, so it's important to remain open to change or your designs will grow stale and formulaic. If something isn't working, or if you've hit a creative block, the best thing to do sometimes is to just scrap the framework you've adopted and try it in a new way. Re-conceiving your methods can save you an enormous amount of time and spare you the frustration of meeting with creative obstacles. I always say that if you hang onto your tricks, secret techniques, and style, those tricks, techniques, and style eventually become prison bars.

I also try to surround myself with examples of great conceptual design. I tear out advertisements from magazines (I found the BIC ad in *Graphis*), and I collect motion graphics like Kyle Cooper's title sequence to *Donnie Brasco* or the recent Volkswagen broadcast spots. And I buy books that feature work of conceptual designers like Stefan Sagmeister's *Made You Look* (Booth-Clibborn Editions) or Steven Tolleson's *Soak Wash Rinse Spin* (Princeton Architectural Press). Having these examples around keeps me motivated to look deeper into conceptual possibilities in my own work.

THIS COLOR IS BLUE!

Look at the small black point in the center of the cross in the orange field for 20 seconds. Then look at the small black point in the grey field. The orange field will appear blue. And that's the way it's meant to be.

On Thursday 3.3.1994 we will open BLUE Clothing stores in Bregenz, Dornbirn, and Feldkirch.

SILENCE
AND A DEEPER SILENCE
WHEN THE CRICKETS
HESITATE

KEEP IT SIMPLE In Hollywood, screenwriters and producers have what they call "pitch meetings" with studio execs in which the writers or producers have to "pitch" their entire idea in one sentence. Known as "pitch lines," these summations provide an immediate means of gauging a story's potential; if the idea can't be expressed in one sentence, it either hasn't been sufficiently thought out or it's too complicated. The pitch line, then, has to be at once simple and comprehensive — basic yet reflective of a broader truth that lurks behind the words used. This requires careful choices and sensitivity to the subtleties of what you're trying to communicate.

Take this haiku by Leonard Cohen:

Silence
And a deeper silence
When the crickets
Hesitate

With just nine words, he articulated both the feeling of being outside on a summer night and the relative nature of silence. The haiku's theme is silence, and the image of crickets chirping is the concept that expresses it. And just as the haiku's beauty lies in its apparent simplicity, so, too, does a good design's.

IN SUM If there's one rule of conceptualizing, it's that there are no rules. I can't think of anything more important in design than good concepts, but laying out a concrete process with which to develop them is impossible. In fact, it goes against the very idea of conceptual thinking. A great idea is perhaps the most invisible aspect of a creative endeavor, and making it visible can often seem like a matter of dumb luck. But in my experience, you have to train yourself to think conceptually, making creative epiphanies more common the longer you practice.

I've found the best way to get started is to simply keep an eye out for great ideas. Read *Adweek* — or better yet, *Adbusters* — study design magazines, and visit sites like DesignInMotion.com. Watch television critically. Think about ads like Volkswagen's "Dome" series or the one for BIC. Try to get inside the creative minds of the people who made them; try to think of how they came up with their ideas. If you're careful, you won't end up copying them. Rather, you'll reach a place in your own mind in which equally unpredictable, unconventional, and brilliant ideas can bloom.

EAT THE AUDIENCE Last summer, I was asked to speak in Toronto at a conference for Canadian book buyers. My publisher set the whole thing up, which was great because I was swamped back in New York trying to finish a design project. Thinking I'd save some time by just using a speech I'd given a few weeks earlier rather than preparing a new one, I relaxed and focused on the work at hand.

A few days later, I endured a nerve-rattling, turbulent flight to Toronto. And looking back, I can't help seeing that turbulence as the ominous foreshadowing of things to come.

As I stood off-stage in the conference hall listening to my publisher give his keynote address just before I went on, I realized that I was about to really embarrass myself. The speech I had under my arm was all about design and inspiration and was aimed at my fellow designers. Everyone in the audience, however, was a book buyer. They weren't at the conference to learn about design; they wanted to know what was hot in digital technology so they'd know what books to stock up on....

But I couldn't back out then, so I got up and gave the speech I'd brought with me. Up on the podium, I knew I was in trouble. I felt like the teacher in *Ferris Bueller's Day Off*, with every point I made being greeted by blank stares. I started to hear my voice drifting out into the room, and the glazed-over faces of the audience so unnerved me that I stuttered and tripped over my words. My delivery got so bad at one point that the organizer tried to cut me off by applauding near the end of the presentation. Needless to say, I was out of there immediately after I finished... running back to New York with my tail between my legs.

On the flight back, after a couple of Sominex and a cocktail, I got to thinking. I recalled a conversation I once had with my mother-in-law, who teaches English as a second language in San Francisco. We talked about how nervous her students get when she asks them to read their compositions. One day, a Japanese student told her that he "eats the audience" as preparation for public speaking. Obviously, the phrase didn't translate very well, but she knew exactly what he meant: He internalizes the audience, considering them in every part of the speech process, from concept to delivery. In other words, the exact opposite of what I'd done in Toronto.

It would have been very easy for me to have avoided the debacle in Toronto simply by doing an hour or two of research. I could have asked my publisher exactly who would be in the audience, and I could have followed that up by locating the theme of the conference, which I easily discovered in retrospect to have been "trends." Instead, I blindly determined that it didn't really matter who the audience was... that a view into our world of design process and inspiration would be fascinating to anyone. Big mistake.

In New Media design it's very easy to make the same mistake. We've all encountered incredibly long downloads of Flash animations or sites that confuse and frustrate us with mysterious navigation. I came across a site recently that issued a proclamation on the load page that warned of long downloads and heavy Flash files. The author proudly stated that he or she "makes no apologies for this and if you don't like it, goodbye." Fair enough. I was gone. Also, we have all probably witnessed the sites, animations, and broadcast spots that seem to be talking to anyone but the target audience, such a site designed for a bank that looks like a teen site, or vice versa. It's surprisingly easy to forget your audience and justify it by waving the flags of "innovation" and "self-expression." I should know, I've done it many times. The problem is that, without fail, the work I have produced while waving that flag has always been less satisfying than work I produce with the audience in mind.

So what are some steps you can take toward including your audience?

ZERO IN Before anything else, we have to know who our audience is and what they want. But because we work on the Web, our audience is basically invisible to us. Without the luxury of seeing them, we have to imagine them in other ways. I do it by creating a kind of composite sketch of my target audience. Like the police do when looking for a criminal, I consider different factors that make the people I'm targeting unique — the subtleties that distinguish them from everyone else. But where police focus on physical details like height and hair color, I think about factors such as their age, education, interests, environment, and the sort of computers they use. And just like a cop's job is made infinitely easier with a sketch of the suspect in hand, our work as designers moves faster and with fewer detours if we know such details about our target audience.

A perfect example of this is the work we did in the summer of 2000 on Web sites and Flash spots for the Backstreet Boys and *NSYNC. Now, my musical tastes run the gamut, from black to white and back again. But nowhere in my vast collection will you find anything by these two groups. Nor do I have anything in common with the audiences they attract, mainly because I've got a solid twenty-plus years on them.

So my team and I started to collect information. We visited fan sites, taking note of their style, the colors and fonts used, and their overall attitude. We bought fanzines, read the press packets the record company had sent us, watched the groups' videos, and listened to their music. We dedicated a notebook to clippings, screen-grabs, stills from various videos, and bits of text and headlines from articles about the bands. With this scrapbook we started to get a feeling for the type of design that would speak to our audience.

Then we considered what types of computers they'd be using. Because our audience was mostly middle-class teenagers, we figured they'd be accessing the sites from home. So we designed the sites to work on any browser using 56K modems, particularly AOL, and with CPUs of 300 MHz. With this technical profile augmenting our already-formed character profile, we constantly checked our work — both stylistically and technically — against our audience as we created the sites.

CLIENT-SUPPLIED INFORMATION Another great source of information about the target audience is your client. This might seem obvious, but it warrants mention here. At the start of any project we ask our client who they are trying to reach, and more often than not we get a very detailed description. In the case of Adobe, for example, we asked them to submit their traffic logs, marketing documents, and any other information or insight they had that would allow us to get to know their users better. Having been in business for close to twenty years, they really knew their audience.

In other cases, with ncw businesses or ad agencies handling a business, we often get a partial picture of the audience. But by asking questions, starting a dialogue, and gathering information, we are able to collectively complete the picture.

FOCUS GROUPS I have worked with focus groups on several projects and had mixed results. Focus groups are composed of people chosen at random who represent the "target" audience. These groups meet in a room and are asked a number of questions about the product and, in the case of interactive design, asked to navigate the site while others watch for areas where the tester gets lost or confused. One problem with focus groups is that they are very expensive and, in my opinion, often lead you straight to the middle of the road. What I prefer to do is invite friends, acquaintances, or, if possible, complete strangers to run our designs by. (We share a studio space with two other firms and I can often entice my loftmates' visitors to test a site or react to a design.) The argument against this is that perhaps third-party focus groups afford you more honest responses because the participants don't know you. This is true, but it is also true that many New Media budgets simply don't have room for a third-party focus group, and collecting your own data is the next best thing. I've developed a sort of "poor man's focus group" to get the same results without spending a dime: I collect my own data. That is, I challenge myself to pay special attention to how I personally respond to what my friends and family say about the designs I show them. If I get defensive about something they say, I try to understand why. If the comment is simply rude or dismissive, that's one thing. But if I feel defensive about a reasonable criticism, I take it to mean that there must be some truth in it... that my subconscious is affirming their critique, and I'd be wise to take it seriously.

IN SUM I think it's easy as a New Media designer to shut yourself off from the whole notion of focus groups or designing for an audience. It's not uncommon for many designers to start to think like fine artists, with their desire to express themselves overtaking the desire to communicate a client's message to that client's target audience. In step two, I talked about the importance of including everyone involved in a given project. Your audience is part of that group. Its members may be physically invisible, existing in your mind only in the abstract, but they're still a fundamental part of your team. Just as it's important to respect your codesigners, clients, and medium, so is it important to respect your audience. As I've said before, graphic designers don't work in vacuums. We all have a unique vision and a unique sense of intuition that, when shared with others, and mindful of an audience, can grow exponentially. Ours is a commercial art, and as such it has to be created for an audience in order to succeed.

BILL VIOLA. STILL FROM "THE MESSENGER" (1996)   Video/Sound installation. As installed in the Durham Cathedral, England.   **Photo:** Kira Perov

FILTER In New Media design, we're always reckoning with limitations: low-bandwidth connections, restrictive color palettes, ever-changing browsers, the inexact science of usability... the list goes on. And it's tempting to see such constraints as enemies of our creative freedom. They often frustrate us to the point where our designs suffer, and worse, we start disliking what we do. But as the saying goes, your enemies are your best teachers, and this is as true in design as anything. That is, limitations can be seen as liberating frameworks that force you to streamline your work, thus making it accessible to the most people possible, both technologically and aesthetically.

At my design studio, we think of limitations as filters. Over the years, and through our mistakes, we've learned to reconsider things that previously annoyed us as welcome editors, keeping us on track from start to finish. We gradually boil our designs down to the essence of what we're trying to communicate, free of any unnecessary frills.

> *Write the story, take out all the good lines, and see if it still works.* — *Ernest Hemingway*

Exactly. Hemingway's writing is revered for its apparent simplicity. His sentences are short and to the point, probably a result of having been a reporter in his youth. But his stories are profound, and their profundity is only strengthened by how they're presented: He sneaks up on you, communicating so clearly that you're drawn in, only to be slowly awed by the great depth that lies behind his simple narratives.

But Hemingway was uncommon. Most artists — be they writers, designers, or musicians — struggle with self-editing. You may include things you believe to be crucial in a design, but those elements are often crucial only to you. In a sense, we're lucky to work with a medium that carries so many limits. It forces us to constantly bear in mind that our designs need to work. And by working, I mean they have to communicate. Again, a wonderful limitation, because beyond having to work, they *get* to work. As designers, we *get* to communicate both visually and functionally.... It's an honor, really, not a hindrance.

FORM Creativity feeds on constraints. It's true that a design's form should follow its function, but that doesn't mean function should erase form. On the contrary, creativity is still a central part of our work; if it weren't, we might as well be actuaries — they make a lot more money. But creativity needs to be focused, and if it's focused effectively, there's virtually no limit to what can be achieved. Think of the great novelists and artists whose geniuses flowered under the most oppressive conditions: Dostoevsky served years in a Russian prison camp; Max Beckmann produced much of his best work during Hitler's campaign to silence and vilify modern artists; Milan Kundera began writing in exile from his native Czechoslovakia; Beethoven composed his Ninth Symphony after he'd gone completely deaf.... Okay, pretty intense examples, but the point is that finding inspiration in adversity is simply a matter of perspective and a willingness to explore new avenues.

One of the most creative sites I've seen recently is for an industrial design company called Fiori, Inc. (http://www.fioriinc.com), which was produced by my friends at Paris France, Inc. — a Web shop in Portland. The site provides a wonderful experience to its visitors. It's simple, yet elegant and aesthetically beautiful. There are no fancy CPU-straining animations or unnecessary elements that cause slow downloads. It consists of just two photos, text, and some vector illustrations. In the section on Fiori's two founders, you click on one of their names to bring up a still photo of the person whose name you chose. There's a small disc — about an inch and a half in diameter — that you move around the screen, revealing text behind the picture about the person. As you move the disc over the image, you learn about the founders and their work through a kind of virtual interaction, mirroring the actual process of getting to know someone.

By respecting the environment for which they were designing, the designers tapped into creative solutions that, without limitations, they might never have considered.

DEMONS AND ANGELS For my money, one of the best films of the 1990s was *Jacob's Ladder*, which tells the harrowing story of Jacob Singer (Tim Robbins), a Vietnam vet living in Brooklyn in the late 1970s. Convinced he's being chased by demons, Jacob is haunted by the past, terrified of the present, and his life quickly degenerates into an existential nightmare. At his lowest moment, near the end of the film, his chiropractor/confidant (Danny Aiello) says to him, "If you're scared of dying, and you're holding on, you'll see demons tearing your life away. But if you've made your peace, the demons are really angels, freeing your soul from the earth."

I know it's a heavy reference, and I'm probably tweaking a few pretension meters out there, but I just don't care. It's a great way to look at things. For designers, the moral translates to this: You can either see limitations as demons tearing your creative freedom away, or as angels freeing you from gratuitous elements and unfocused designs. Again, it's all a matter of perspective.

FROM THEORY TO PRACTICE: THE 60-SECOND MOVIE
As with many things, filtering is easier said than done. So last year when RollingStone.com asked us to produce a series of movies about different musicians to be streamed on the company's Web site, our conviction was really put to the test. We talked with the folks at RollingStone.com about their audience and the general nature of the Web, and decided to limit the length of these movies to 60 seconds. While 60 seconds is an eternity compared to how long many New Media spots last, our task was still a daunting one: How could we capture the essence of any musician's life, vision, and spirit in 60 seconds? And to do it so the spots could be streamed easily over low-bandwidth connections only added to our anxiety. But it was too interesting an idea to pass on, so we took it.

The first band on the list was the New Jersey-based metal act Monster Magnet. We were excited about working with such a colorful band, and that excitement got in our way. First, we decided not to use tripods, opting instead for a handheld, jerky look. This, of course, only created more information

on the DV tape, since both the subject and the camera were moving. Ultimately, we had a hard time compressing the files, and the picture quality turned out a little shoddy.

Our second mistake was in the editing. I thought it would be cool to use a blurred shot of a moving subway as a transitional effect. This again affected the picture quality. With Web-based video, the faster or more sudden the motion, the harder the compressor has to work, leading to low resolution.

Finally, in another act of overzealous artistry, we used slow-motion footage of the band in concert. The video was shot at the standard video frame rate of twenty-nine.97 frames per second, but after compressing it for the Web our frame rate was 15 frames per second. Cutting the frame rate by almost half turned the already slow footage into nothing but a sloppy, stuttering mess.

Fortunately, Dave Wyndorf, the band's lead singer, was charismatic enough to overshadow the mistakes we'd made, and the spot turned out okay. But we wanted the next spots in the series to be more than okay.... It was time to "take out all the good lines...."

The following feature was on the smoky-voiced, ex-Fleetwood Mac sensation Stevie Nicks. One of my longtime favorites, Nicks has a quiet, assured demeanor; and her music exists on another plane, if not another planet than Monster Magnet's. So a more austere approach was necessary anyway, but given the problems we had with our first attempt, we knew the spot had to be simple for technical reasons as well. So we securely fastened our camera to a tripod, took time to ensure proper lighting, and replaced the fancy title edits with a black screen and white text — and we didn't use a trace of slow motion.

The result was exactly what it was supposed to be: a clean, uncluttered feature on Stevie Nicks. No gratuitous animations or special effects distracted from the focus, which was to present as deep an impression of Ms. Nicks as possible in 60 seconds. We befriended the Web's limitations and produced a spot that was not only more focused than the first, but one that looked and performed better.

IN SUM I believe strongly in the power of filters. I believe strongly in designing for the environment. I simply cannot justify heavy downloads... it makes me feel like a failure if I can't design a site or a motion spot that actually works in its environment. In the case of the Web, that means whatever I design shouldn't make people wait, it has to play on at least last year's CPUs, and if it's interactive it has to be intuitive. My design has to "work." I feel that I have this opportunity to communicate using both graphic design as well as the way the design performs. They work in tandem to present an experience, and I can't take either for granted.

It's a very personal thing for me. I'm not suggesting that it's right for everyone; but for me, respect for the delivery medium is elemental and essential. Respecting the medium is a wonderful opportunity, because the limitations placed on me as a Web designer, or as a broadcast designer for that matter, actually serve me in ways I never expected when I started my career. I rely on limitations — whether bandwidth, CPU power, client directives, or time — to strip away... to filter non-essential elements from the design.

JUSTIFY August 2001: I'm on a plane, flying to Las Vegas for a job, headphones on, cranking whatever MP3s I have on my hard drive, trying to quell my fear. The plane is bouncing around, dipping, and rattling. In the middle of it all, I recall a line from some pop song — "Nothing really matters..." — and I weave that phrase into my white-knuckled prayers. But when I'm in the worst of it, it occurs to me that the line is crap. Watered-down Zen Buddhism. In fact, everything matters. The plane and everyone on it matter; the clouds matter; the birds below matter. Las Vegas, New York, and every town in between matter. My company, coworkers, and work all matter... And most important, my wife and little boy *matter*... a lot.

Clearly, the experience brought out the philosopher in me. And it's a philosophy I hold in every aspect of life, including my work. But with one key difference: In life, everything is important, no matter how small or seemingly insignificant; in design, each element must be deliberately chosen, and only then does it matter. In other words, every last thing doesn't count unless it directly serves the design's function. Which brings me to the final chapter of this section and the last step of our process: Justify.

EVERYTHING MATTERS I've said it countless times, I know, but it's important enough to say again: Design is a functional art form. As such, it relies on a certain minimalism. Not that all design is minimal, of course; it's just that everything counts. Each design has a singular, often very simple purpose, and there's no room for extraneous features that only digress from that purpose, whatever it may be. So you have to constantly make value judgments and justify them as you go. Anything you can't account for is a waste of time, money, or space, and often of all three.

To use an earlier example, when we designed the interstitial for 3Com's HomeConnect DSL service, we made sure that everything — the bright palette of red and white, the fast zooms and pacing, the fonts — reflected the theme "fast and easy." The spot animates fast, and it's simple in design. And because each element so clearly embodies that theme, I don't have to verbally justify them. But I could if someone asked.

Still, being able to explain each element isn't always necessary. Sometimes a design can only be understood intuitively, and its elements transcend verbal explanation. Our spot for the Manifestival digital film festival, for example, communicates its themes clearly, but I can't really say how or why. I know each element demands to be there, and I know the design wouldn't work as well if any were missing. But I can't verbally explain each element's function, which is likely what makes me an artist and not something else; I communicate visually and make decisions intuitively, but they're decisions nonetheless. And as long as I'm honest with myself and open to criticism, I believe those decisions can be trusted.

JUSTIFY AS YOU GO The best way to stay on track and not waste time is to continually question your design decisions. When I started redesigning our corporate site in late 2000, I was lost. Earlier that year, I'd published my first book, *Flash Web Design,* and I'd been delivering keynotes on Flash at design conferences all over the place. Both helped cement (perhaps even over-cement) my reputation as a Flash designer. So naturally, I felt extraordinary pressure to create a kick-ass Flash site for my own company in order to showcase both my skill and belief in the technology.

I sought out sites I thought were amazing and bookmarked them to use as references while I worked. At the top of the list were requiem-foradream.com (the site for Darren Aronofsky's 2000 film) and soulbath.com, an experimental art piece — both created by Hi-Res!, a design studio in London. Another favorite was Brand.New (http://www.vam.ac.uk/vastatic/microsites/BrandNew_Site/flashframe.html), a great commentary on commercialism designed by Siegelgale. I also kept a close eye on leaders in the Flash community such as Matt Owens, Todd Purgason, Fred Sharples, and Josh Ulm to keep up with the cutting edge. I was inspired by everything I found but was struggling with my own site.

I mocked up five different Flash-authored comps for potential home pages and shared them with our creative director, Ian Kovalik. Ian is very polite, but when it comes to creative direction, he doesn't beat around the bush. He had the same criticism for each comp I showed him, confirming my gut fear that I was consistently missing the mark. I'd developed a reputation as a Flash designer, and I knew what I liked in others' work, but I couldn't seem to get it right on my own site. So what was wrong?

I was letting the "cutting edge" detract from what I really wanted the site to communicate: my company's core values. I was allowing sheer possibility to override my beliefs in form, respecting the medium, and speaking to the head via the heart through design. I was overzealous and unfocused — a terrible combination in a creative person.

Then something wonderful happened. Ian and I were going over my latest comp, and I was demonstrating how to navigate it. Ian watched, paused for a second, and asked, "Why do you have rollovers?" This pissed me off, and I got defensive. I'd put a lot of time into designing and then implementing what I thought was pretty impressive Flash work, and I was angry that he was questioning it. But the very fact that I was so upset validated his criticism, which I only realized once I'd calmed down a little. The rollovers had no purpose. In fact, they hid valuable information behind their complexity. You had to roll over the main navigation buttons to see the subnavigation choices behind them, and there weren't enough of those to justify the rollover. In other words, they only hurt the design. So why use them at all?

I sketched out a navigation system that displayed both the main links and the subsection links on one page, and it was perfect to me. The global navigation became clear and intuitive, and it didn't require plug-ins or JavaScript to use. Ian was essentially saying, "Justify the rollovers," and I couldn't do it. Once finished, the site wasn't the striking Flash 5 opus I'd imagined. Instead, it was simple, minimal, and beautifully functional. And it got there by Ian or myself constantly asking ourselves and each other to justify each element as we designed.

IT'S NOT ALWAYS IMPOLITE TO POINT When we get close to finishing a project, we call a meeting. Everyone gathers around a monitor and whoever is leading the project presents the work. At this point, anyone can point to anything on the screen and say "Justify." Thus we impose a final filter as a group, each of us bearing in mind that every color, move, and font should support the design's theme. While we may let a few unjustifiable elements slide in the name of creativity, for the most part we're pretty ruthless about keeping the design as streamlined as possible. Of course, these sessions usually include a few fistfights, but they're worth it. In the end, the designs are as clean as they can get, and everyone's happy.

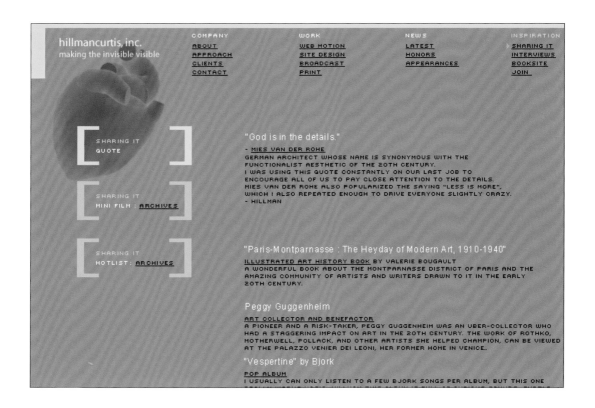

IN SUM This step is a perfect example of how our process is often nonlinear. Justifying as we work is as important as justifying the end result. It saves us time, money, and energy for future projects. It's especially linked to filtering. In a way, they're the same step; they just present different ways of going about it.

If you work with a team, justifying is simply a matter of communicating with your co-creatives and remaining open to their comments. A fresh set of eyes can often identify unnecessary elements instantly. If you work solo, it may take time to train yourself to objectively assess your designs, but it's possible. Whatever the case, it's important to remember that we're artists and we need to allow for some intuitive flexibility. Not everything can be rationally explained. Still, if something — whether it's your logical mind, your gut, or a coworker — is telling you something isn't right, pay attention. Because if you can't justify a move, or a font, or a color choice to yourself, the work won't ring true to you… and that's a feeling, in my experience, you want to avoid at all costs.

INSPIRATION

MTIV: INSPIRATION In the winter of 2001, I gave the creative keynote speech at the flashforward conference in San Francisco. My talk was all about finding inspiration to fuel your creative vision. At the time, I honestly thought I would be booed... Well, maybe not booed, but have a bunch of walkouts. That was ridiculous considering the supportive Flash design community, but I felt that way because I wasn't talking about Flash, or, for that matter, ActionScripting, the scripting component of Flash software, which was the big buzz at the time. Instead, I had drawn up a talk based on finding inspiration — everywhere — and using it to influence your own work, regardless of the software or even the medium. I thought the people in the audience would want how-to tips and techniques and would find my talk about inspiration pretentious and disappointing.

I showed up a few hours early to do an equipment check, sort of a dress rehearsal, and was amazed at the size of the stage and venue in general. I was told the conference expected somewhere around 2,500 people... which was terrifying to me at first. But I remember thinking that if nothing else I would be talking about something that I believed in, and more importantly, something I knew was elemental to design.

This section of the book is based on the talk I gave that day. And the talk itself grew out of a simple practice of sharing we have at the studio.

It worked like this: If I was reading a great book — say, *Making Movies* by Sidney Lumet, (Vintage Books) — I would hand it to our creative director, Ian Kovalik, as soon as I was done. He would then read it and hand it to Homera. Or perhaps Grant would come in, and, as his computer was starting up, turn and say to me, "Did you see the Viola show up on 57th Street? It's amazing," at which point I would shake my head in disbelief, ashamed that I wasn't aware that there was a new Bill Viola show. I would recover quickly enough, though, to mention the Philip-Lorca diCorcia show at the Pace/MacGill Gallery in SoHo. And so on.

The point is that, in our small shop, we're always collecting inspiration and sharing it with each other. We then use those shared inspirations as starting points, like blueprints or maps, for our own work. Sometimes we even find ourselves using them to directly communicate our ideas, suggesting "a little Kyle Cooper" (*Donnie Brasco,* not *Seven...*) here, and "a touch of Brockmann" there. And always, always chanting that classic Hemingway line, "Write the story, take out all the good lines, and see if it still works" as we go.

What I hope to make clear with this section is that we are all, as creatives, trying to do the same thing. That, regardless of our medium, whether it be design, poetry, fiction, painting, filmmaking, or any other form of creative expression, at the core of everything we do lies the need to communicate.

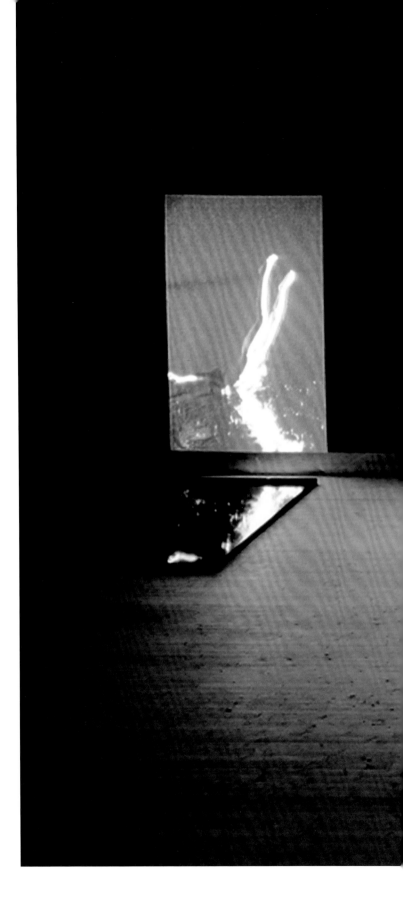

WHAT'S IN A WORD So what is inspiration? The Merriam-Webster dictionary has several definitions, but two in particular really stand out for me:

The action or power of moving the intellect or emotions.

In other words, you experience something, and it speaks to you. In the best of cases, it moves us to respond creatively. We want to add to or continue the idea. Walking home one day after work, I passed the Yohji Yamamoto store on the corner of Mercer and Grand in SoHo and noticed these great posters featuring their clothes. I stopped and studied them for a while and everyday after that when I passed the store I looked at them again. They were photos cropped at odd angles with blocks of black and bold white lettering. The effect was arresting and suggested excitement and youthful vigor... at least to me. At about the same time I was trying to figure out how to design and treat a new video featuring the band Sum 41. The visual inspiration I got from the Yamamoto posters was the answer. The posters moved me enough to respond. The slashed and fragmented look of the posters was perfect for this young band loaded with punk energy.

The act of drawing in, specifically the drawing of air into the lungs.

This definition is perfect, because without inspiration we cannot move forward. It is the air we breathe to fuel our creative progress. And I believe this is the best way to look at everything inspirational around us... never as anything but air we breathe in, letting the work that makes us take those deep breaths go straight to the heart. Inspiration fuels every piece of work I do. My starting point is usually a page from a design magazine, or a film I love, or a quote from a book, or a poster in a storefront. I start with the inspiration I find anywhere I can and that becomes my fuel.

Many years ago, I heard a designer lecture on the topic of how one finds ideas. He suggested a book titled *Techniques for Generating Ideas* by James Webb Young (NTC Business Books, NTC/ Contemporary Publishing Group) and said it was a simple, straightforward way to do just that. I bought it immediately, dove in, and came up emptyhanded. It has sat in the studio's bookcase, untouched, ever since. This experience made it clear to me that we don't generate ideas. Ideas/inspiration are all around us and, like air, we share them — breathing them into our bodies and returning them, changed, into the creative atmosphere.

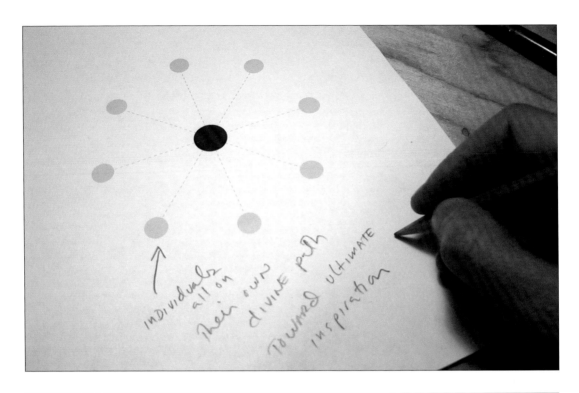

individuals all on their own divine path toward ultimate inspiration

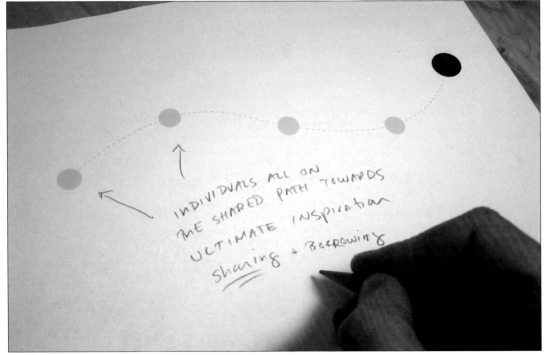

INDIVIDUALS ALL ON THE SHARED PATH TOWARDS ULTIMATE INSPIRATION sharing + borrowing

THE MYTH OF DIVINE INSPIRATION In preparing for my speech at the flashforward conference, my coworkers and I started talking one day about epiphanies — those inspirational flashes that come seemingly out of nowhere — and drew a diagram to illustrate the idea.

But in talking more and looking at the diagram, we started to question the direction we were moving in. We agreed that we had all, at some point, felt divinely inspired. But upon deeper reflection, we concluded that before such moments occurred, we'd actually been seeking out inspiration, often unconsciously. Ultimately, though, we were always working toward inspiration.

> *It was in that room too that I learned not to think about anything that I was writing from the time I stopped writing until I started again the next day. That way my subconscious would be working on it and at the same time I would be listening to people and noticing everything...* — Ernest Hemingway

So we talked some more and came up with a new diagram. We discussed inspiration and where it comes from, what fuels our creative energy, and even why we became designers in the first place. As we talked, it became clear that we, as creatives, are walking a shared path, strewn with the ideas of those who have walked it before us. We felt that once on the path, we couldn't help but pick up some of those ideas on our way.

CREATIVE GENIUS But, you may ask, what about works so great, so original, and so monumental that they couldn't be the result of anything but divine inspiration? Take Pablo Picasso's 1907 painting of a Parisian brothel, *Les Demoiselles d'Avignon*. To look at the piece, which marked the beginning of Cubism, whatever inspired it was nothing if not divine. How, during a time in which art had just barely begun to stray from straight representational form, could he have conceived such images? Women fragmented, their figures flattened into planes seen simultaneously from different angles, no identifiable environment to provide any clues to the work's meaning. Nothing in all of western art even remotely resembled this new style, so it's tempting to think Picasso was plugged into some realm beyond anything earthly.

Through a little research, however, you learn that in 1906 the artist had come across a collection of African masks in the studio of André Derain, a fellow artist and his neighbor in the Montparnasse district in Paris. The masks, traditional and ancient, inspired the angularity of the women's faces. You also learn that the painting's unusual palette — its burnt oranges, earthy yellows, and muted browns — was inspired by Henri Matisse, another contemporary and neighbor. Picasso was clearly tuned into his environment, taking in knowledge and ideas everywhere he looked, allowing them to inform his own creativity. And out of that indirect and nebulous collaboration grew one of modern art's most significant periods, forever rooting Picasso in the great world history of art.

I begin with an idea, and then it becomes something else. — Pablo Picasso

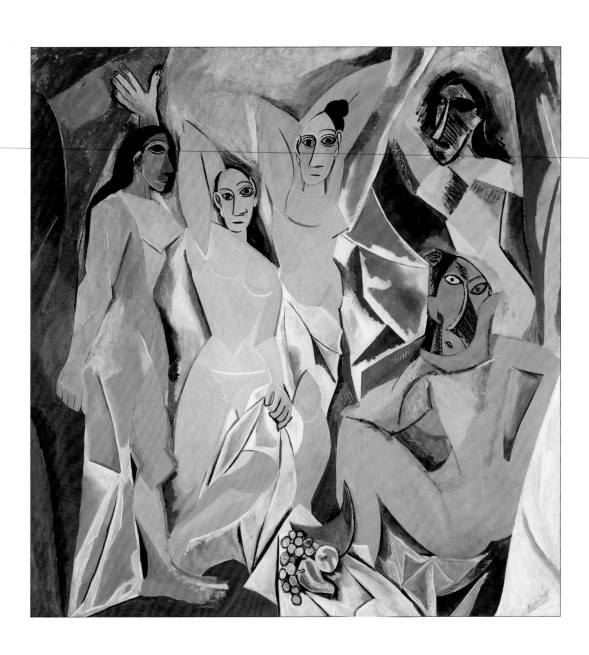

THE FIRST STEP But there's still no question that Picasso was a genius, and unfortunately we can't all claim the same for ourselves. So how do the rest of us begin? For me, it's always the same: self-doubt. We've all stared helplessly at blank computer screens, sketchpads, or canvases from time to time, and inspiration is nowhere to be found. In its place is what I call the Bad Voice. It's the one you use to beat yourself up, to make yourself feel worthless. For me, it always says the same things: "Hillman, you're a fraud. You have no real ideas. Give it up."

I think every designer feels worthless from time to time… obviously I do. But by identifying this feeling as a necessary first step toward my ultimate inspiration, I can get through it with less anguish. By giving it a name and a purpose, I can recognize it not as an impasse but rather a hurdle that I've jumped many times before.

LOOKING EVERYWHERE Once I've gotten past the self-doubt and all its trappings of self-consciousness, I can begin looking at the work that surrounds me — even if it's so good I can't help but feel threatened or is of a different medium than anything I'd use — and see the potential inspiration in it.

I have seen you, beauty, and you belong to me now, who ever you are waiting for and if I never see you again, I thought. You belong to me and all Paris belongs to me and I belong to this notebook and this pencil. — Ernest Hemingway

Hemingway understood the cyclical nature of creativity: the process of taking in, of inhaling the world, letting it mingle with his own creative spirit, and then exhaling something new that would, in turn, become part of the external world for others to inhale. Simply put, whatever inspires us belongs to us. And the work we produce, then, belongs to our surroundings.

Another great story that exemplifies my point is one I read once about the great collagist and painter Robert Rauschenberg. During his formative years in New York, Rauschenberg would frequent two bars: one full of visual artists like himself; the other with dancers, choreographers, and musicians. After splitting his time between the two for a while, he gravitated more and more to the second bar. He said he was inspired by the energy of the people there and the music they listened to. And before long, he began to see their influence in his paintings.

I love this story because I've always responded to the rhythm and movement of Rauschenberg's work. Knowing that his unique vision was so much informed by another medium inspires me because it means that he was open to any inspiration he could find... that he was aware of the commonality of creative expressions.

MY METHOD In any given week, I'll visit a gallery, buy or borrow a few CDs, see a couple of movies, and study my favorite movies on DVD. I'll read art history, film theory, fiction, and poetry. And, of course, I immerse myself constantly in design books and magazines. It's all part of my ongoing effort to draw from the work of others. Finding in design books, perhaps, great starting points; or from movies or their titles, blueprints; or from poems or fiction, maps to follow. I'm not plagiarizing or stealing but borrowing and returning. I'm engaged in a dialogue among myself, the work that inspires me, and the world in which I live.

FALL IN LOVE WITH A MASTER In the beginning months of 2001 I was banging my head against a wall trying to come up with a suitable direction for our site redesign. I had tried everything I could think of and had actually designed one version almost to completion. But each comp I designed failed under the weight of its own ambition. I felt pressure to design a site that would blow people away and erase any memory they might have of our original site design.

My thought was to design something bold and cutting-edge, so I studied the work of my peers: designers who I thought were doing new and exciting work. Still nothing was working. The designs I turned out really fell flat, and every night I went home empty and depressed.

Finally, one night at home, my wife Christina was sharing with me some of the highlights of a poetry conference she'd just attended. It was called the Dodge Festival, and it's sort of like Woodstock for poets — minus the brown acid. Of the many readers and lecturers she heard, C. K. Williams really made an impression on her, as he would soon make on me as well.

A member of the audience asked the poet what he does when he's creatively blocked, when he can't start the next poem. Williams responded without hesitation: *I fall in love with a master.* Instead of immersing himself in the work of his peers, he explained, he looks further back, to those who perfected their craft long ago, to those who originally inspired him to write poetry when he was a young man.

Listening to Christina tell this story, I knew I'd found my answer. While much of the work I was looking at was impressive, none of it was speaking to me at the very core. So the next morning, I hit the book collection in my office and zeroed in on the design legends: Saul Bass, Paul Rand, Tibor Kalman, Ikko Tanaka, Paula Scher, and Pablo Ferro, to name a few. Then I came across one of my all-time favorites: Josef Müller-Brockmann.

The Swiss designer, who established himself during the '50s and '60s, used complex grid structures for his beautiful, often minimalistic posters. I've always been drawn to the stability and consistency in Müller-Brockmann's work and how every color, line, and font seems to be the product of careful consideration. So after flipping through the book (*Josef Müller-Brockmann Designer: Pioneer of Swiss Graphic Design,* Lars Müller Publishers), I knew I'd found my model.

I wanted my site to exhibit the same thoughtful functionality, thus buttressing my longstanding belief in always finding the simplest solutions to design challenges and to use that simplicity to allow subtle, often deep beauty to come forth. So we designed, with help from our friend, the designer Ben Wuersching, a grid system upon which to lay out and design our site.

God is in the details. — Ludwig Mies van der Rohe

This quote, from one of the 20th century's most important architects, became our war cry during the redesign process. As we worked, we started to believe with evergrowing conviction in the power of details. We began with the idea that to your naked eye, a pixel difference from page to page may be invisible, but to your subconscious, it wouldn't. You would be slightly aware of the imbalance, and it would register within you and cause some discomfort. From there, we didn't let any detail slide. We demanded of ourselves as fine-tuned a site as we could create — from pixel to pixel, byte to byte, and page to page.

And though no single page of the site will ever "blow you away," the system of the site, where elements appear in the same places from page to page, where navigation is consistent and immediate, and where information is presented clearly, started to shine with a sublime beauty to us.

dienstag, den 7. januar 1958
20.15 uhr großer tonhallesaal
12. volkskonzert
der tonhalle-gesellschaft
zürich
als drittes konzert
im zyklus «musica viva»
leitung hans rosbaud
solisten alfred baum klavier
andré jaunet flöte

schweizerische erstaufführungen
andré jolivet
cinque danses rituelles
ernst krenek
zweites klavierkonzert
luigi nono
«y su sangre va vienne cantando»
musik für flöte und kleines orchester
bernd aloys zimmermann
sinfonie in einem satz

karten fr. 1.-, 2.- und 3.-
vorverkauf tonhallekasse hug
jecklin kuoni
genossenschaftsbuchhandlung

musica viva

J. Müller-Brockmann

Gestaltungsprobleme des Grafikers
The Graphic Artist and his Design Problems
Les problèmes d'un artiste graphique

Gestalterische und
erzieherische Probleme in
der Werbegrafik –
die Ausbildung des
Grafikers

Creative Problems
of the Graphic Designer
Design and Training in
Commercial Art

Typographie, dessin, photo,
labels, couleurs, etc.

Verlag Arthur Niggli Ltd.
Teufen AR Schweiz

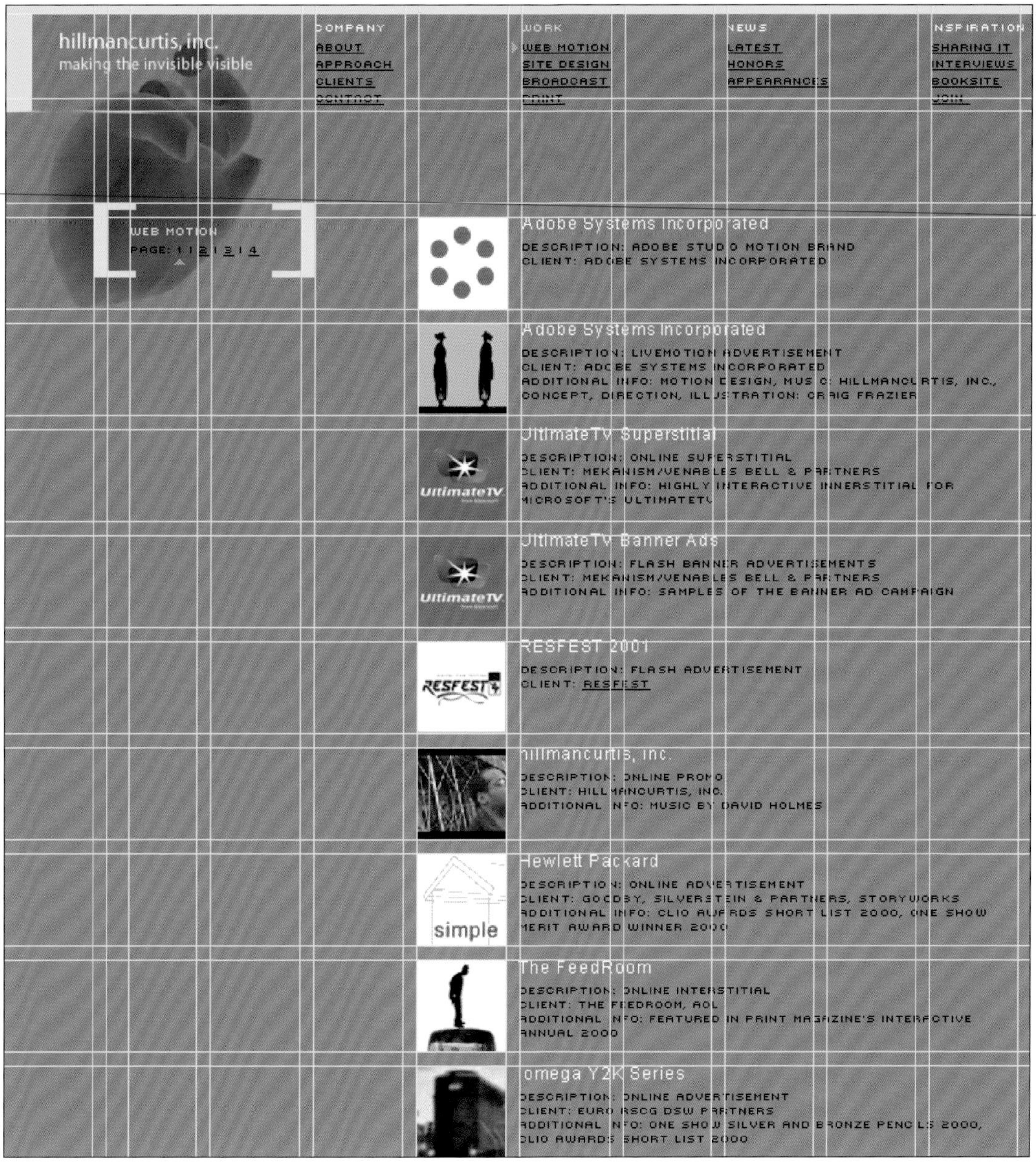

COMPANY
ABOUT
APPROACH
CLIENTS
CONTACT

WORK
WEB MOTION
SITE DESIGN
BROADCAST
PRINT

NEWS
LATEST
HONORS
APPEARANCES

INSPIRATION
SHARING IT
INTERVIEWS
BOOKSITE
JOIN

WEB MOTION
PAGE: 1 | 2 | 3 | 4

Adobe Systems Incorporated
DESCRIPTION: ADOBE STUDIO MOTION BRAND
CLIENT: ADOBE SYSTEMS INCORPORATED

Adobe Systems Incorporated
DESCRIPTION: LIVEMOTION ADVERTISEMENT
CLIENT: ADOBE SYSTEMS INCORPORATED
ADDITIONAL INFO: MOTION DESIGN, MUSIC: HILLMANCURTIS, INC.,
CONCEPT, DIRECTION, ILLUSTRATION: CRAIG FRAZIER

UltimateTV Superstitial
DESCRIPTION: ONLINE SUPERSTITIAL
CLIENT: MEKANISM/VENABLES BELL & PARTNERS
ADDITIONAL INFO: HIGHLY INTERACTIVE INNERSTITIAL FOR
MICROSOFT'S ULTIMATETV

UltimateTV Banner Ads
DESCRIPTION: FLASH BANNER ADVERTISEMENTS
CLIENT: MEKANISM/VENABLES BELL & PARTNERS
ADDITIONAL INFO: SAMPLES OF THE BANNER AD CAMPAIGN

RESFEST 2001
DESCRIPTION: FLASH ADVERTISEMENT
CLIENT: RESFEST

hillmancurtis, inc.
DESCRIPTION: ONLINE PROMO
CLIENT: HILLMANCURTIS, INC.
ADDITIONAL INFO: MUSIC BY DAVID HOLMES

Hewlett Packard
DESCRIPTION: ONLINE ADVERTISEMENT
CLIENT: GOODBY, SILVERSTEIN & PARTNERS, STORYWORKS
ADDITIONAL INFO: CLIO AWARDS SHORT LIST 2000, ONE SHOW
MERIT AWARD WINNER 2000

The FeedRoom
DESCRIPTION: ONLINE INTERSTITIAL
CLIENT: THE FEEDROOM, AOL
ADDITIONAL INFO: FEATURED IN PRINT MAGAZINE'S INTERACTIVE
ANNUAL 2000

omega Y2K Series
DESCRIPTION: ONLINE ADVERTISEMENT
CLIENT: EURO RSCG DSW PARTNERS
ADDITIONAL INFO: ONE SHOW SILVER AND BRONZE PENCILS 2000,
CLIO AWARDS SHORT LIST 2000

una rivista che parla del resto del mondo **a magazine about the rest of the world**

COLORS

13

warning: this magazine contains no words. start here ▶

attenzione:
in questa
rivista non ci
sono parole.
comincia qui ▶

Arg 3 pesos | Aus 4.95A$ | BRD DM6.50 | Can 4C$ | Esp 450Ptas | Fr 20FF | Hellas 750DR | HK HK$35 | India Rs.100 | Ire IR£2 | Ital L6.000 | Mag 250FT | Mex 9$ | Nederl 7,95FL | Port 520$00 | SA 9R | UK £2 | USA $4.50

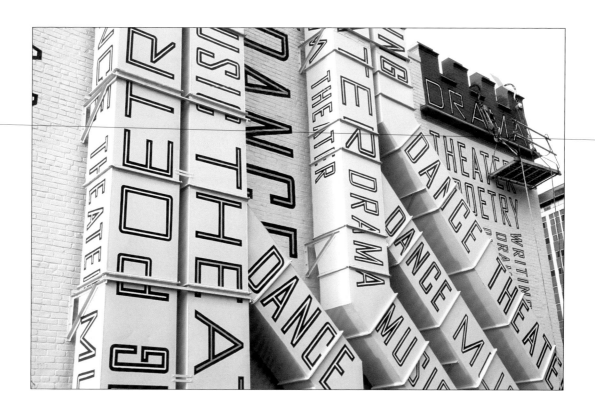

This page: **IKKO TANAKA, NOH PLAY "THE 5TH KANZE NOH" (1958)** © Ikko Tanaka Design Studio   Opposite page: **BARBARA KRUGER Untitled (It's A Small World But Not If You Have To Clean It),** 1990 Photographic silkscreen on vinyl 143 x 103 in. The Museum of Contemporary Art, Los Angeles Purchased with funds provided by the National Endowment for the Arts, a Federal Agency, and Douglas S. Cramer.

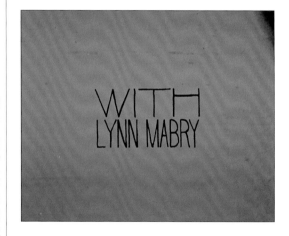

STILLS FROM "STOP MAKING SENSE" (1984)　Title Design: Pablo Ferro　A film by Jonathan Demme & Talking Heads.　Courtesy: Pablo Ferro

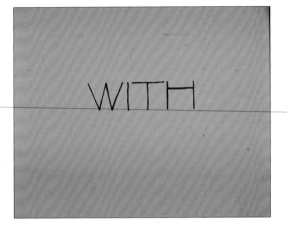

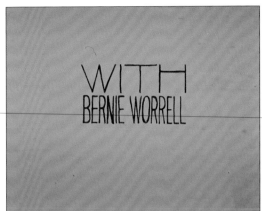

HONOR THY CONTEMPORARIES But falling in love with a master doesn't mean you should ignore your contemporaries. As I mentioned earlier, Picasso was as influenced by Matisse's palette as he was the African masks in Derain's studio.

Before becoming a graphic designer, I was an "almost famous" rock musician in San Francisco. I played guitar and sang for two bands that both got record deals, but each one dissolved before anything really took off. I learned a lot during those years, but the most valuable lesson was never to close your eyes to potential inspiration. In other words, don't let pride prevent you from seeing the greatness in others, even if they're your direct competitors.

The last band I was in was very close with another group that practiced in the same studio as ours. We ran in the same circles, played the same clubs, and even shared band members. They were signed about the same time we were, but to say they went further than we did would be a drastic understatement.

During the early years, before their stardom, I was intensely envious of their talent and the following they'd already developed in San Francisco. It was irrational, really, because they were among the most supportive and encouraging people I've known, but I still couldn't shake my envy. I became so competitive that I stopped enjoying their incredible live shows and demo tapes. Instead, I just grew critical and standoffish.

One day, after hearing that I was having trouble writing new songs, their lead singer offered to help me out. We even set up a time to meet in the studio to write a song together. But at the last minute, I called and cancelled the session. I didn't want to admit that I needed help or that he was a better songwriter. I was so shut down by competitiveness and envy that I killed an opportunity for what could have been a great experience.

A year later, my band had gotten nowhere, and his was on the cover of *Rolling Stone*. Of course, this isn't to say that if I'd met him that day, my band would have made it too. It's just to point out that by letting my envy get the best of me, I ruled out an experience that, at the very least, would have given me a glimpse into how a great songwriter works, and at the most, a hit song.

So when I found my calling in graphic design a few years later, I vowed never again to bind myself up with such competitiveness. Naturally, I still feel my chest tighten a bit when I see amazing work coming out of others. But instead of being critical and trying to find fault in their designs, I promote them. At conferences, I'll often show the work of design firms such as Sagmeister, Inc.; Tomato; Tolleson Design, Inc.; Pentagram Design; Juxt Interactive; Number 17; and countless others. I promote them because I respect them but also because it does wonders for my own psyche to turn envy into inspiration. No matter how successful we become, we're never above that.

I've never avoided the influence of other people. I would have regarded that as cowardice and a lack of self-confidence. — Henri Matisse

The next few spreads are a few examples of people who have influenced me. These designs, some of which were created by competing firms, inspire me for many reasons; but I'll let the work speak for itself.

This page: **STILLS FROM SOULBATH.COM** **Design by:** Hi-Res! London **VIDEO STILLS FROM THE FILM NEWPORT** **Design by:** David Hartt and Gary Breslin **Design by:** Kontruktiv.net © Matt Anderson 2002
Opposite page: **SCREENSHOTS FROM THE MINIML.COM SITE** **Design by:** Craig Kroeger © 2001 miniml.com **STILLS FROM FAKTUR/A**

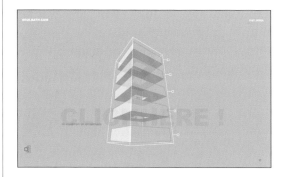

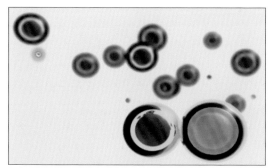

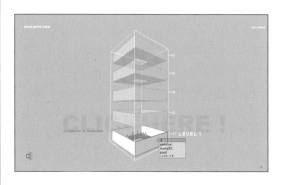

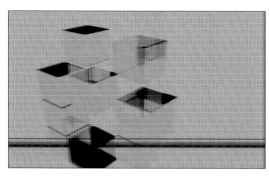

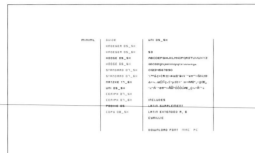

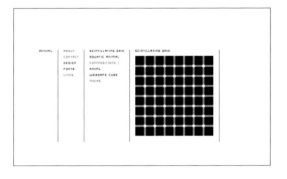

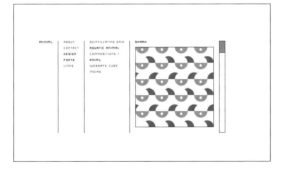

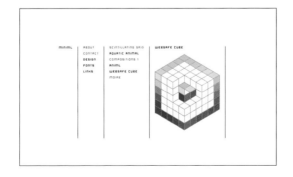

THEME = STYLE In Sidney Lumet's book *Making Movies* (Vintage Books), there's one passage that comes back to me every time I sit down to work:

> *The question 'what is this movie about?' will be asked over and over again throughout this book. For now, suffice it to say that the theme (the what of the movie) is going to determine the style (the how of the movie)... I work from the inside out. What the movie is about will determine how it will be cast, how it will look... and, with a good studio, how it will be released. What it's about will determine how it is to be made.*

That's it. These words, written by a filmmaker, confirm for me one of the central tenets of my own design philosophy: Theme = Style.

As I discussed in "Theme," our work on the Adobe Studio site exemplified this philosophy. Before we even turned on our computers, we sat down with Adobe's creative team and talked about the theme behind the new offering. We talked about how it would serve the design community by allowing people to share ideas, inspiration, and techniques with each other. Then we started talking about how to represent those ideas in a brand logo and after experimenting with various approaches, we landed on a design we called "Spark." Symbolizing both community and inspiration, this design was the clear winner — its style carries the theme of Adobe Studio in every detail.

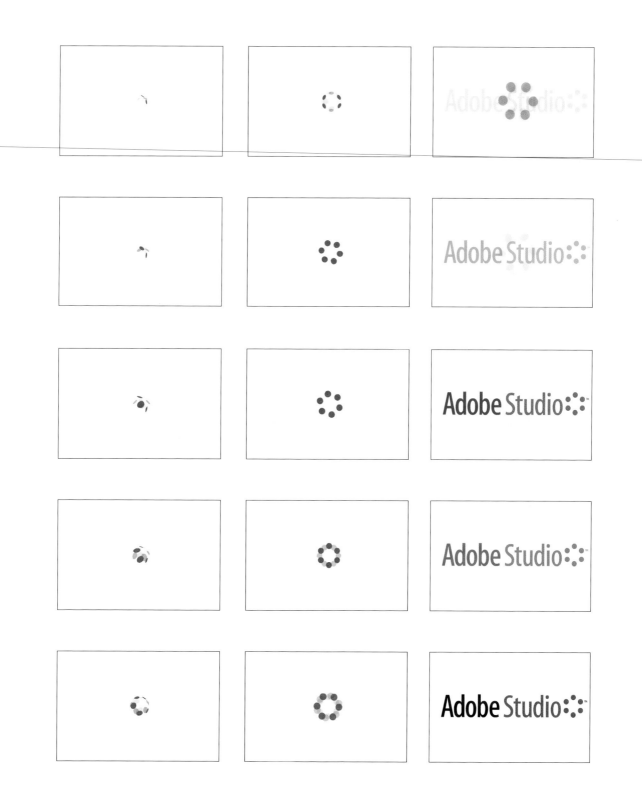

TELL THE STORY THROUGH CUTS Like *Making Movies*, another book I often read for inspiration was also written by a filmmaker: *On Directing Film* by David Mamet (Penguin Books). Long known for his hard-hitting, psychologically complex screenplays, in the past decade Mamet has become a highly significant director. His montage style is austere compared to the work of many other filmmakers, and it's a style he's chosen deliberately. He explains his aversion to the handheld method of following actors around, regardless of how uninteresting or insignificant their actions are to the story. Instead, he thinks each scene through and sets up only those shots that will directly serve the film's narrative.

Both Ian (our creative director) and I read the book and loved it. Shortly thereafter, we combined his theories with Lumet's use of tight shots to build a foreboding sense of claustrophobia in shooting a DV spot for one of our clients. So the style of the video was itself a montage — a little Mamet, a little Lumet, and a little Ian and myself. We took in the inspiration, let it mix with our own ideas, and created something new. And the result was better than anything we'd have come up with completely on our own.

Write the story, take out all the good lines, and see if it still works.

A line I've already praised many times, this advice to writers also showed up in Mamet's book, furthering my belief in the shared path of creative people. Taking out whatever you as the creator think are the most impressive elements is one of the hardest things to do. But clearly, David Mamet, like me, believes it's the only way to create truly good work.

If I started to write elaborately, or like someone introducing or presenting something, I found that I could cut that scrollwork or ornament out and throw it away and start with the first true simple declarative sentence I had written. — Ernest Hemingway

Just as Hemingway begins with the first true sentence, I'm always thinking of ways to minimize the space between my message and my audience. I remove all the ornamental hurdles — anything, no matter how cool, that might just get in the way.

In late 1998, I was asked to design a Flash movie to promote a new John Lennon box set for Macromedia and Capitol Records. During one of the initial meetings, someone mentioned that Yoko Ono would be reviewing the piece and giving it her stamp of approval — or not. I was a little intimidated; but more than that, being a big John and Yoko fan, I felt compelled to design something that would really impress her.

I created one comp that I felt pretty good about, but it was really busy. After listening a few times to the song that would accompany the piece — Lennon's version of "Happy Christmas (War is Over)" — it became clear that I'd missed the mark. As one of the 20th century's most influential artists, Lennon wrote songs that redefined popular music, crossed boundaries, and made us question ourselves. He died tragically and prematurely, and his memory is sacred among the millions who still revere him. My design was simply too distracting.

So I started "taking out all the good lines." Out went the big 3D elements, the extraneous text, and everything else that just obstructed the message of the simple song and the great musician. I pared the spot down to just three basic elements: the song, a self-portrait Lennon had sketched, and a photograph of him. The only animation I used was to have the sketch slowly morph into the photo, a subtle but effective accompaniment to the song.

I felt good about the design, and fortunately, so did the client.

MAKE A PLACE One of the great New York modernists, Mark Rothko is best known for his colossal, abstract color-field paintings. The large blocks of reds and oranges, blacks and yellows, and blues and greens fill huge canvases with their simplicity. But despite how basic they appear, his paintings are unmistakably profound, eliciting in their viewers a powerful emotional response most works of art never do. How Rothko achieved this was simply a matter of approach. He once said,

They are not pictures. I have made a place.

What a wonderful quote. I related to it immediately because I sometimes feel that it's easy to fall into a pattern where you are designing beautiful pictures that never really take you anywhere. Sort of like sending a bouquet of roses with no note attached. My goal is always to try to design a place. Sometimes I'm successful, other times not, but the Rothko quote is perfect because you don't want just a picture. You want to take people somewhere with your designs. One of my all-time favorite film titles illustrates this perfectly. It's the opening to the film *Donnie Brasco.*

It starts with a close-up of Johnny Depp's eyes, hooded, looking down. And slowly, through a series of still images, the eyes open. They are the eyes of a predator... We've seen this very shot in nature shows: the wolf or lioness crouching, eyes full and directed, silently watching, waiting to attack the weakest member of the herd. Depp's eyes nearly fill the screen. The footage is all black and white. Finally, after a slow crescendo, a line of text appears on one of his eyelids. Nothing fancy, just a simple fade-up, a ghost flutter or two, and the text sets into place.

The start of this sequence is perfect for a few reasons. First, it's absolutely beautiful. The framing is wonderful, calling to mind the predator image, and also paying homage to Saul Bass's title sequence for *The Man With the Golden Arm,* thus joining a long line of motion graphic expression. The pacing is perfect as well, lingering on the closed eyes for almost too long before they open, as if from a deep sleep; but their alertness reveals not a sudden awakening, but the patience of a stalker. Add the silvery, muted tones of the footage and the subtle fade-up of text, and I dare you not to be as drawn in as I am. Because in these first moments of the film, more than a story has been introduced. Kyle Cooper, who designed the sequence, has made a place.

SAY IT CLEARLY... One of the best things about acknowledging the shared path we all walk as creative people is that we often find inspiration in the most unexpected places. While I was writing this book, my wife was getting her MFA in creative writing. One of her teachers was the great American poet Marie Howe, and to Christina, Ms. Howe was a real mentor. She recommended to my wife many wonderful, often esoteric, difficult writers to read.

One night after dinner Christina mentioned that Marie had introduced a new poet to her. His name was Bruce Weigl, and he had received a Pulitzer Prize nomination in 1988 for *Song of Napalm* (Atlantic Monthly Press), a book of poems drawn from his experiences as a soldier in Vietnam. The poem that Ms. Howe introduced to Christina, titled "The Impossible," was not from that collection, nor was it based on wartime experiences. Rather it was a personal, confessional poem that recounted a tragic and disturbing experience from, one assumes, Mr. Weigl's childhood. In it, Weigl writes in a sparse and clear style of meeting a drifter who leads him to an empty trainyard and molests him. As Christina read it to me that night, I found myself becoming uncomfortable and annoyed. I resented the poem... harsh and unflinching, and resisted it. I felt the author was deliberately making his poem shocking and disturbing... until the last line:

Say it clearly, and you make it beautiful, no matter what.

As soon as I heard that line, the full weight of the poem just fell on me, washed over me, and the resentment and anger I had felt lifted, and for a moment I couldn't talk. With that one line the poem suddenly became a testament to the power of art.

By writing clearly, Weigl was shining the beautiful light of his craft upon an experience almost too painful to recount. My wife told me she felt the poem was what is called an Ars Poetica, which is a poem about poetry, and I felt I understood what Weigl was doing. In effect, he was saying, *with dedicated and careful writing, I can create something right from something that was wrong. With my craft, I can reconstruct small parts of my world — however terrible — and make them beautiful.*

And I was grateful. I took a deep breath, repeated the line in my head, and decided that it would become mine. I would apply that line to everything I set out to design.

IN SUM Our job is not an easy one. It takes tremendous dedication and patience to become and remain successful in any creative field. We spend our days thinking of new ideas; we don't have the luxury of checking out mentally if we get tired and working on cruise control until our energy returns.

But as hard as being creative can sometimes be, its rewards are worth every bit of the effort. And to know that we're not alone, that countless others have followed and continue to follow the same difficult path, comforts me. I know that I can learn from them, whether they're alive or dead, musicians or poets, filmmakers or designers. I know their work came from the same place as my own: from deep inside their subconscious, their environments, their world of influences, and their friends. Like mine, their creativity is at once only partly their own and entirely their own and entirely my own. It comes from a kind of collaboration with others and their works that span time, genres, and mediums. They are my partners, just as I am theirs, and they are each other's.

But to say it clearly, it's my belief that inspiration exists everywhere. We simply have to remain open to it, regardless of where we find it and the form in which it comes. The path we walk is only as rich with inspiration as we allow it to be.

NEW MEDIA DESIGN is a new frontier. It's like the Wild West — full of pioneers who've traded their old professions for the wide open space of new possibilities. And as all pioneers do, we in the field must learn as we go, remain open to change in order to survive, and never let arrogance overcome us. We must allow surprises and those little bits of wonder to guide and inspire us; it's the only way to move forward.

And I should know; when I started out in design, I was lost. I knew nothing of typography, grids, and color. In fact, I knew virtually nothing about technology. I remember once, when I was still a musician, one of my bandmates had to explain to me the difference between a computer's hard drive and its memory — and it still took me a while to get it.

But I was compelled to learn, so I began reading, attending classes, and experimenting. I learned by making flat-out mistakes, guessing, and receiving the generous wisdom of my coworkers over the years. I learned by listening and taking advice. And the best part is that I'm still learning.

Because many of its technologies are constantly evolving, in a sense New Media will always be a level playing field. Beginners and longstanding designers alike are always on the cusp of a new era, always faced with new tools and challenges, and always prone to the same mistakes and victories. So whether you're just starting or hoping to learn a new trick to use on a project for a major client, I think there will be something in this section that will help you.

The nine chapters run the gamut of issues facing New Media designers today: typography, color theory, XML, Web layout and languages, streaming video, grids, usability, and more. While some introduce the latest technologies, others cover the fundamentals of design. But I encourage you all to go into each chapter with an open mind to what their authors have to share. Because I've found that no matter how much I think I know about even the most basic aspects of design, I can always learn more.

I asked my design peers — all of them experts on the topics they've covered — to write the chapters in this section for a couple of reasons. First, I thought it would be a wonderful and helpful addition to the book, and I wish I'd had something like it when I started out. Which leads to my other reason: I still believe I can learn from others now as much as I could as a beginner. And I can tell you that after reading these chapters, those areas where I felt my knowledge was a little fuzzy have become much clearer thanks to the insights of these distinguished designers.

It's as much an honor for me to include these essays as it is exciting. I hope that in some way these essays will inspire you and perhaps assuage fears that may be holding you back from exploring a new medium.

ELLEN SHAPIRO ON GRIDS

Ellen Shapiro is a graphic designer, writer, and design educator based in Irvington, NY. The author of the book Clients and Designers *(Watson-Guptill, 1990) as well as many articles in design magazines, she teaches at SUNY Purchase College and the University of Baltimore. She has developed and is marketing a line of learning materials based on multisensory teaching methodologies that help parents and teachers help children, especially those with learning disabilities, learn to read. See http://www.alphagram.com.*

THE ART OF THE GRID The grid is back. Its future wasn't always secure. In the '90s it looked like the Deconstructionists, hell-bent on unpredictability, were going to beat out the Modernists, for whom Swiss-inspired clarity was the Holy Grail. The debate officially began in 1991, when gridmaster Massimo Vignelli called *Emigre* magazine "garbage" and "an aberration of culture." By 1995 one could hardly open a design publication without getting caught in the crossfire between "the chaos of the new aesthetics" and "the prison of the grid." Since then, *Emigre* has become an icon in design history, and today it's hard to find award-winning examples in design annuals in which deconstruction and unpredictability are the motivating factors. A multiplicity of design styles peacefully coexist. By and large, chaos is out. Structure and simplicity are back.

The grid, according to Philip B. Meggs in *A History of Graphic Design* (John Wiley & Sons, 1998), was first seen in the early 1920s in Bauhaus-influenced books designed by El Lissitsky. The grid turned the printed page from something akin to a blank canvas, on which anything goes, into a framework akin to the structural support system of a building. The grid reached its apex in 1960s and 1970s Swiss-International Style. Designers who rigorously adhered to strict grid systems, using few typefaces and ample white space, achieved what they considered, timeless perfection of form.

THE BASICS OF GRID CONSTRUCTION Ironically, the computer, which made possible the experimentation Vignelli called "vulgar" and "confused," forced designers back into the grid. Or, more accurately, software, not the computer itself, reinstitutionalized the grid. To build a document, you have to make choices that are similar to drawing up a page framework with drafting tools. In The *QuarkXPress 4 Book* (Peachpit Press, 1998), David Blatner admonishes designers to build a document with mathematical precision and then place elements on it with creativity: "First you decide on specifications — how tall and wide, whether it's double or single-sided, and so on," he writes. "Then you build the structures of the page — page elements that repeat,

page numbering and text flow. If you don't do these steps first, the foundation of your work will be unreadable — and your building might just fall down."

HOW I LEARNED TO LOVE THE GRID I learned about grids early. My first graphic design experiences (although I hadn't heard the term *graphic design* at the time) were on the junior high school yearbook staff. It was 1962, the year John Glenn orbited the earth in the Friendship 7 space capsule. In Mrs. Schottland's art room at George W. Crozier School in Inglewood, California, a dozen other thirteen-year-olds and I pasted up pictures of the band, the football team, and the student council with scrapbook-like abandon, each picture overlapping the next. Pictures were any size, any angle. Every page was different, photos mixed with text and with our "original" drawings and cartoons. By the time I became editor of the high school yearbook, I had, courtesy of *LIFE* magazine, discovered the grid. I didn't know that term, either. But by studying my parents' magazines I discovered the underlying structure that allowed *LIFE*'s art directors to create an infinite number of variations within a page organization system. With the intensity with which other girls studied lipstick colors and hairdos, I studied how the pages in *LIFE* were divided into vertical columns; how heads, pictures, and other elements were hung from horizontal guidelines, more or less invisible to the reader; how text was rhythmically interspersed with photographs; how bleed photographs added drama. The pages of the 1966 Inglewood High School yearbook were laid out on a grid drawn with ruler and triangle on our kitchen table.

Thirty-six years later, after working with page grids of every ilk, I am trying, with mixed success, to apply grids to Web design. For a print veteran like me it's not so easy. Unlike the printed page, nothing wants to stay put. A page seems fine in Netscape on the Macs in the office; when I look at it in Explorer on the PC, everything has changed: the font, the type size, the position. A few years ago, after moving from New York City to the suburbs and falling in love with gardening, I had fantasies of a second, weekend career as a garden designer — until I learned how quickly deer, insects, drought, rainstorms, and a host of other uncontrollable factors can wreak havoc with the most carefully planned compositions. Web design often seems more like garden design than print design. Yet in its own way, the Web grid is even stricter than the magazine, newspaper, or brochure grid. One of the charms of print design is the ability to break the grid, to place a picture or another element over the line, creating unexpected visual interest. A good print designer develops the underlying structure, then plays with it and "violates" it. Theme and variations, as in Bach's *Art of the Fugue*, make exciting brochures. The requirements of "tables," however, make Web design much trickier.

GRIDS ON THE WEB Web design, the new baby in the designer's repertoire, is an exciting, boundless form. But because HTML was initially devised as a way to display ASCII text in a pleasing manner, it's somewhat limited in what it can display. The "table," a systems of rows and columns, came into being to organize text and data on the screen. Then developers and programmers realized they could use it as a tool to place objects, including images, at exact locations, regardless of the operating system or browser. To make a table work, however, you have to manipulate the objects to fit it; and often you have to compromise their sizes or slice them. This may change in the future with the upcoming XHTML and DHTML standards and browser support. Until then, to build a site that is accessible to the average user, easy to navigate, and provides instant access to information, you've got to respect the limitations of the tool. Of course, there are tricks of the trade that make the "grid-and-table" look disappear, but underneath it all, the grid is there.

LOOK TO THE MASTERS It's unfortunate that most design students today don't get at least some training in precomputer-era design techniques. But they've been using computers since age three, and their hands and heads know how to use a mouse, not drafting tools. However, much can be learned by studying exemplars of the art. Here are a few of my favorites.

TAYLOR'S GUIDES These tall, slim gardening guides (*Taylor's Guide to Perennials, …to Vegetables, …to*

Taylor's Guide to

Orchids

More than 300 orchids, photographed and described, for beginning to expert gardeners

Herbs, and so on), published by Houghton Mifflin and designed by Massimo Vignelli, are an object lesson in how grids can make complex information beautifully understandable. Vignelli helped coin the title "information architect," and these reference books, bibles for the gardener, illustrate how a publication designer can base diverse sections (essays, color plates, plant encyclopedias) on an intelligent, flexible grid system, much like an architect places the different functional parts of a building within its framework.

THE WILLIAMS-SONOMA CATALOG This catalog has 158 pages of theme and variations perfected by Kit Hinrichs of Pentagram, arriving with regularity in your mailbox. From stockpots to fine china, cheeses to cleaning supplies, every page holds a delicious surprise, whether it's a tomato-shaped pot that breaks the grid or a recipe artfully placed behind silhouetted products. The classic but never boring grid allows for vertical columns as well as many-sized rectangles in which merchandise can be displayed. "Most cataloguers base their layout decisions on a square-inch profitability analysis," explains another of Hinrich's catalog clients, Kathy Tierney of The Nature Company (which is now a part of Discovery Store). "Kit takes something like a pot-holder and makes it four times bigger than a product costing many times more. We're never boring because we never do the expected or the mundane." See the Williams-Sonoma Web site, too.

ESQUIRE Is it good writing or good design that makes this magazine so worthwhile? Both. *Esquire* design director John Korpics and staff bring us a monthly package of innovative typography and art direction. The Web of delicate horizontal and vertical hairline rules — and the way the type and pictures are shoved up against those rules — is especially noteworthy. Look at (and read) "Fidel and the Magic Boy" in the September 2001 issue. Exquisite writing, illustration, typography, use of color… and a magic grid that holds it all together.

METADESIGN.COM This site is one of the best demonstrations of what makes well-structured interactive design equal to but different from print design. Flash animates the grid and makes it sing and dance, but quietly. The red background, which might not work in a printed brochure, sets off the elegantly simple typography and the icon-based interface. Metadesign founder Erik Spiekermann, partner Terry Irwin, and staff demonstrate the ideal marriage of design and technology.

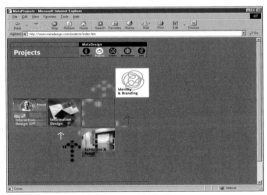

THE SHAPIRO COURSE ON GRIDS If I were to assign exercises to help students learn how to appreciate and use grids, they might be something like this:

1. Gather together text and pictures on a subject that interests you. The text should be about 2,000 words in length, and the pictures should be of various sizes, in both black-and-white and color.

2. On a large piece of drawing paper or illustration board, using a T-square and triangle, rule up an 11 x 17-inch horizontal rectangle. Divide it into two 8.5 x 11-inch vertical pages. Draw margins at 3 picas at the top and outside edges; 4 picas at the inside gutters and bottom. (It's important to design in picas, because picas and points are the units of type measurements.) Divide each page into four equal columns with 1.5 picas between columns. Use your calculator and pica ruler. Divide the column into four equal vertical spaces and draw horizontal lines across the pages.

3. Set text type at the column width you specified. Place large tracing tissue over the board and begin laying out the type, taping down the "galleys" with Scotch tape. Design three or four spreads: some with all type, some with type mixed with pictures, and some with mostly pictures. All type must fit in the columns. Pictures must be one, two, three, or four columns wide. All elements must "hang" from one of the horizontal rules. Vary the pages as much as possible within the structure. Think syncopated rhythm.

4. Design three or four more spreads, but start deconstructing the page by breaking the grid. Change the sizes and widths of the type columns. Make the elements sing and dance. Do more interesting things with the pictures, like silhouetting some of them — yet with the grid still underneath as a guiding framework.

5. Now try this exercise with three-column and five-column grids on different size pages. Notice how different grids might work better for different kinds of material, even within the same publication. For example, in a college catalog, the pages with general descriptions of schools and programs could be on a two- or three-column grid, and the pages with course and faculty listings could be on a five-column grid.

6. Do the same thing on the computer, in QuarkXPress or PageMaker.

7. Redesign the same material for the Web in a horizontal format, including an interface with tabs or buttons and other navigation devices.

FOR FURTHER STUDY Professionals and students who want to know more about grids can reference these classics: *Grid: A Modular System for the Design and Production of Newspapers, Magazines, and Books* by Alan Hurlburt (John Wiley & Sons) and *Grid Systems in Graphic Design: A Visual Communication Manual* by Josef Müller-Brockmann (Ram Publications).

A well-illustrated resource for interactive designers is *Web Style Guide: Basic Design Principles for Creating Web Sites* by Patrick J. Lynch and Sarah Horton (Yale University Press), found online at http://info.med.yale.edu/caim/manual. To quote the authors, "The goal is to quickly establish a consistent, logical screen layout, one that allows you to 'plug in' text and graphics for each new page without having to stop and re-think your basic design approach.... Without a firm underlying design grid, your project's page layout will be driven by the problems of the moment, and the overall design of your Web system will look patchy and visually confusing."

LEATRICE EISEMAN ON COLOR

Leatrice Eiseman is a color specialist who has been called "America's color guru." In fact, her color expertise is recognized internationally, especially as a prime consultant to Pantone, Inc. She has helped many companies, from small one-person startups to large corporations, make the best and most educated choice of color for product development, logos and identification, brand imaging, Web sites, packaging, point of purchase, interior/exterior design, or any other application where color choice is critical to the success of the product or environment.

She heads the Eiseman Center for Color Information and Training and is also executive director of the Pantone Color Institute. Lee is the author of four books on color, including, Colors for Your Every Mood *(Capital Books, Sterling, VA)*, which was chosen as a Book of the Month Club selection and received an award from the Independent Publisher's Association. Her newest book, Pantone Guide to Communicating with Color *(published by Grafix Press, Ltd.)*, is distributed by North Light Books, Cincinnati, Ohio.

She delivers many color seminars and is widely quoted in publications such as Elle Decor, House and Garden, HFN, Harper's Bazaar, Vogue, People Magazine, Communication Arts, Graphic Design USA, Consumers Digest, Wall Street Journal, New York Times, Los Angeles Times, USA Today, *and* Advertising Age, *as well as numerous other trade and consumer publications. Lee has made appearances on CBS, NBC, ABC, CNN, MSNBC, HGTV, Discovery Channel, and the FOX network in the U.S. as well as abroad and has been interviewed by radio s tations worldwide.*

If you're interested in exploring color even more, check out http://www.colorexpert.com.

COLOR THEORY (or at least my take on it!) Is there anyone today, especially in the world of design and/or marketing, who doubts the importance of color? We have learned how color adds value and meaning to communication, giving life to the visual message, intensifying it, making it more identifiable and important. The thoughtful use of color can increase the speed of comprehension for the viewer, establish character, and produce instantaneous associations that are more easily recalled.

Often the visual message is all there — language, images, and colors. As to color in the commercial world, especially on a Web page, a would-be client or customer can't touch or feel the product (or service), can't smell it, and certainly can't taste it. So the visual message has to suffice, and that is where color really delivers.

From the dawn of civilization, essential tribal, political, religious, and artistic education has been achieved through a visual language that includes the significant use of color. Humans have always been fascinated with and curious about the phenomenon and origin of color. Endless grade school class projects have included experiments that pass sunlight through a prism, resulting in magical rays of color that spill forth. We can thank Sir Isaac Newton for his original 17th-century experimentation that ultimately gave scientific evidence to the origin of color and its connection to light. (It was his vast range of experimentation that earned Isaac his esteemed "Sir.")

In his classic treatise, *Opticks*, he defined his visual process: "The rays, to speak properly, are not coloured. In them there is nothing else than a certain Power and Disposition to stir up a sensation of this or that Colour. So Colours of the object are nothing but a disposition to reflect this or that ray more copiously than the rest." (In those days, they were big on flourishes and capital letters.)

Modern science recognizes that colors are actually caused by waves, and it is the difference in the length and number of vibrations of those waves that determines the various hues and shades of the spectrum: red, orange, yellow, green, blue, indigo, and violet. Rainbows provide the most magnificent examples of spectral order, with red having the longest wavelength and violet the shortest. Again, Sir Isaac displayed his brilliance by joining the colors together into a circle. Talk about a winning design!!!

When the waves of light enter the eyes, they produce the sensation of illumination and color. It's actually a bit more involved than that, but simply stated, when a leaf appears green it is because the surface of the leaf reflects green rather than because it is green. The earth is brown, the sea is blue, some flowers yellow, while others are red because, when struck by light, they each reflect a specific color and absorb all other colors. End of story... Well, almost.

FIGURE OUT THE THING THAT COLOR DOES Being the complicated creatures that we are, our reactions go well beyond the physical phenomena. There is another very vital dimension to the perception of color, and that is the psychological response. If lavender appears lighter than purple, it is purely a sensory occurrence. It is simply what we see. But if lavender suggests a feeling of nostalgia or romance, then psychological reactions are brought into play.

We respond to color psychologically on several levels; the first and most important is by association. Word association studies utilizing color samples demonstrate a similarity of responses based on certain givens. Show most people a sample of a specific blue and they will almost invariably respond with the word "*sky.*" Distinct shades of blue will evoke still other associations, notably "*sea,*" "*water,*" "*clean,*" "*calm,*" and the temperature will be perceived as *cool.*

Conversely, show most people an example of a true red and they will connect it to fire, blood, excitement, and/or danger. The temperature is definitely hot. These kinds of reactions are subliminal and, most often, cross-cultural. Some responses are based on a collective unconscious, "*ancient memory,*" as it is called, coming from deeply rooted associations to color that are passed on from generation to generation, while others are learned through training, cultural background, and/or environment.

DON'T TAKE COLOR SO PERSONALLY Individual responses to color will also emerge from very personal experiences, most often those that occurred during childhood. And these will vary from person to person. You may dislike green intensely because it reminds you of the color of the half of a worm left in the apple that you had taken a big bite out of when you were in the third grade and you were thoroughly repulsed by the yuckiness of it all! Yet at the same time, you know that green is undeniably the color of foliage and is pervasive in the natural world around you. You might allow your more emotional response, generally based on negative associations long since past, to overtake the more rational and positive response. As a professional dealing with color, it is extremely important to divorce your personal likes and dislikes from your professional judgment.

You know how frustrating it can be to deal with a client, boss, or coworker who has had almost irrational responses to a color that, in your judgment, would be the perfect shade for a specific application. My advice is to educate yourself as best you can in the psychological aspect of colors so that you can effectively pass this information on to coworkers and clients, in order to help them overcome their prejudices. When I teach programs in color, the first thing I ask my students to do is to take a color word-association test so that they can delve more deeply into personal responses to color and learn (I fervently hope) to be truly objective.

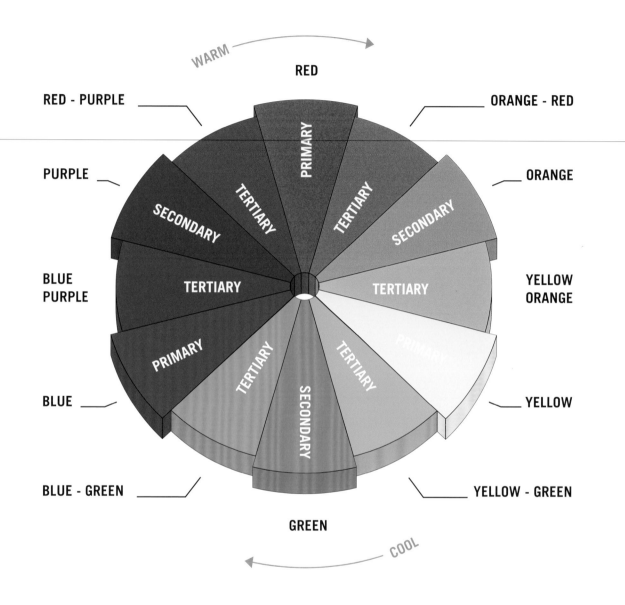

WARM

RED

RED - PURPLE

ORANGE - RED

PURPLE

ORANGE

PRIMARY

TERTIARY

TERTIARY

SECONDARY

SECONDARY

BLUE
PURPLE

TERTIARY

TERTIARY

YELLOW
ORANGE

PRIMARY

PRIMARY

BLUE

TERTIARY

TERTIARY

YELLOW

SECONDARY

BLUE - GREEN

YELLOW - GREEN

GREEN

COOL

DETERMINE THE TEMPERATURE Getting back to Sir Isaac's color wheel… Although we most often think of it as a color placement tool that is very helpful in creating combinations, it very graphically displays one of the most fundamental aspects of color psychology — the association of color temperatures: the cool colors (blue, green, blue-green, and violet families) versus warm colors (red, orange, and yellow families) mentioned previously. Obviously, the image of a product or a concept must jive with the preconceived notions of warm and cool. Whether online or on the store shelf, a refreshingly cool drink would seem totally out of context and even confusing to the person viewing that product if it appeared in red or orange packaging.

But it is dangerous to overgeneralize on the temperatures, remembering that changing an undertone of a color can alter the perception. For example, blue-reds are cooler than yellow-reds; red-purples seem hotter than blue-purples; yellow-greens are viewed as warm while blue-greens are seen as cooler.

The color wheel can take us beyond psychological meanings into the physiological. Before your eyes start to glaze over as you think this is turning into a college-text chapter, let me simply give you the example of complementary colors (also referred to as *complementaries*) on the color wheel and the resulting effects. Note the spelling is *complementary* with an *e* in the middle and not an *i*. In color parlance, complementary colors literally "complete" each other; red is never redder than when it is paired with shades of green; blue is at its bluest juxtaposed with tones of orange; purple literally shimmers when placed next to yellow.

Place two vibrant complementaries next to each other and they seem to vibrate along the periphery of the area where they meet. No special effects, nothing magical — simply a physical phenomenon that involves the scientific aspect of color.

KNOW THE QUESTIONS The questions for the designer remain: Do I want the message to vibrate or do I want to create more subtlety? What am I trying to sell to the viewer? Should I shout to gain their attention, or will a more subtle approach be more in tune with the intended message?

When more subtlety is desired, the complementaries can be reduced in intensity or brightness. For example, instead of a vibrant red-purple and brilliant yellow-green, substitute a deeper red-purple and a mid-toned khaki-green. And if an even softer message is desired, a lighter red-lavender juxtaposed against a misty green would be an effective combination.

Contrast is paramount where legibility is a factor. While complementary schemes offer good contrast, contrasting values of any specific color can offer contrast as well. In color terminology, *value* simply means the degree of lightness to darkness of any color, depending on the amount of light that a hue reflects. The use of black against white or vice versa is the most obvious example of basic contrast. Closely related values are calm and noninvasive, creating soft edges between them, while sharp changes in value create more drama.

The *saturation* level or *vividness* (often referred to as *chroma*) of a color is an important consideration in design as it describes the intensity of a color: how much or how little gray it contains. The purer a color, the more saturated it becomes. At full saturation, the hue reflects boldness, clarity, and truth. The grayer and more neutral a color becomes, the less its saturation level. Descriptive words for less saturation are *muted*, *subdued*, and *toned down*. The grayed-down tones offer a visual relief in contrast to the brights.

The emotional reaction to a hue is greatly altered by its value or saturation level. So it's not just about color families and the messages they impart; it's also about the nuances of contrast. It is always important to remember that colors are rarely used in isolation, so the effect of the color sitting immediately adjacent can make or break the intended message (as in the example of the complementaries mentioned previously).

How do you know if a color combination is right or wrong? In the world of expressive color (as is all color), there are few absolutes such as nevers, always, and must-nots. In my books and seminars I use the word *guideline* and assiduously avoid the word *rules* because creativity or gut feelings might be stifled — and for designers, and no matter what the medium, that's not a good thing! There are times when you are testing the color possibilities, particularly when working on the computer, where color is all about light and reflection, and some wonderfully innovative combinations will emerge.

The last century has literally witnessed an explosion of color brought about by the access to more information and exposure to increased use of color through the creative arts, architecture, interior design, fashion, textiles, film, television, photography, advertising, packaging, consumer products, and, of course, the computer. As color is so much more pervasive in their environments, people have become more accustomed to it. It becomes an integral part of their everyday lives. They are rarely shocked by it unless it is used so far out of context that they are repelled by it. (Think of eating a green hot dog!!) As a matter of fact, they have come to expect color in their world, and, just as when they were children looking to express their innermost feelings with a box of crayons, they will inevitably be attracted to colorful messages.

KATHARINE GREEN ON TYPE

Katharine Green is the Director of Corporate Communications at Zyvex Corporation, the first molecular nanotechnology company, and the VP of Corporate Communications for the Texas Nanotechnology Initiative.

Prior to joining Zyvex in March 2000, she spent three years as Creative Director at Macromedia working directly with Hillman Curtis on the redesign of the corporate Web site (which won a Webby Award in 1999). Recognized as an authority on branding, Green was responsible for co-developing Macromedia's award-winning corporate identity with Neville Brody. The packaging designs won numerous awards, including: Print Regional Design Annual's Best Packaging of 1998; Step by Step Design Annual's 100 Best Designs of 1998; and Publish Magazine's *Best Software Packaging of 1998. Previously, Katharine was Macromedia's Senior Product Manager for Fontographer and the FreeHand Graphics Studio. She has also held positions as Creative Director and Director of Font Development at Altsys Corporation.*

SO you have over a hundred fonts on your computer, and you'd like to use them all. There are script, cursive, block, and decorative faces. Bold, plain, and elaborate styles. Wouldn't a page with all of them as a background look cool? A virtual smorgasbord of fonts? Maybe... but my advice to you is this: don't do it! There are only a few designers who can pull this off. If you aren't one of them... don't do it.

But whether you are creating a page of text graphics or a simple page of bullet listings, it's important to know how to use type correctly if you want to make your message clear. There are many more books on the subject of typography, some of which are listed at the end of this chapter, but here are the basics.

FONT FACES There are many styles of type designs. To name just a few: script (Brush and Freestyle), glyphic (Fritz Quadrata), display (Block and Ironwood), slab serif (Syntax), transitional (Janson text), and Venetian (Centaur). For the purposes of this chapter, we will just focus on the two basic styles, serif and sans serif.

SERIF Serif typefaces have little extensions (serifs) on the arms, stems and tails of characters. Some examples of serif fonts are Times, Palatino, and Garamond. Serifs were originally designed to lead your eye from one character to the next. For this reason they are great when used for correspondence, user manuals, and brochures (in other words, anytime you want to make it easier for your reader to read a lot of text).

Serif

However, serif typefaces aren't always the best choice for text on the Web.

SANS SERIF Sans serif means (literally): without serifs. Examples of sans serif typefaces are Arial, Helvetica, and Optima.

Sans serif faces are generally used for headings.

SANS SERIF

But on the Web, especially at smaller sizes, sans serifs are great for text. Take a look at this example to see what I mean:

Marshall McLuhan theorized that "The medium is the message," proposing that the means used to communicate a message is more important and has more impact than the message itself.

Marshall McLuhan theorized that "The medium is the message," proposing that the means used to communicate a message is more important and has more impact than the message itself.

Both fonts are the same point size. While you would mostly likely use the bottom example (Times Roman) in print, you would definitely use the upper example (Arial) on the Web and on presentations that will be viewed on a screen.

You do have a moderate amount of control with HTML text, as seen from a Web browser. You must call several sans serif font styles in the HTML code that reference fonts found on both Macintosh and Windows systems. These specific fonts are Verdana, Arial, and Helvetica. The HTML script you need to use is: <font face="Verdana, Arial, Helvetica, sans-serif" size="1">

Take care not to combine serif typefaces in both headings and body text. The example below illustrates this point quite well.

Serif Heading

I'm using Garamond for the text in this paragraph. I love Garamond. But, in this case, the text conflicts with the heading.

Sans Serif Heading

I'm still using Garamond for the text in this paragraph. But now, I am using a sans serif typeface that compliments the body text... instead of competing with it.

FONT STYLES There are four basic font styles: plain, bold, italic and bold italic. The ones we'll cover here are bold and italic.

BOLD Professional typographers design a special font for other styles and weights of a typeface (like bold and italic). This is done so that you don't have to rely on your computer's algorithms to "fake" the weight your bold font should be. Take a look at the example below.

Arial
Arial
Arial Black
Arial Black

The first font is the standard Arial. The second font, Arial Bold, has actually been bolded by the computer.

However, if you look at the first example of Arial Black, you will see the font designed for use in bold headlines. The second example of Arial Black is the Arial Black font after it's been bolded by the computer. You can also see how the character spacing has changed in this version. In some cases the space inside the letters starts filling in as you bold the character. For the best result, use the bold version of the typeface that the typographer designed.

ITALICS Italic characters slant to the right. They are best used to set off quotes and special phrases. However, they generally don't do well when used on the Web in small sizes. Save these for large text as shown below.

"Italics are great for quotes."

Type designers create special characters for an italic typeface. If there is no italic version of the font, your computer will create its own version, which is actually an oblique, or right-slanted, typeface (without the special characters). Note the difference in the oblique version of Times Roman in the first example and the actual italic version of the typeface in the second example.

Use italics sparingly
Use italics sparingly

You can see obvious differences in all the characters, but especially in the r, y, i, and the a.

HANGING PUNCTUATION Hanging punctuation can be used for characters such as periods, quote marks, commas, semicolons, and bullets. It emphasizes your quote or point. Look at the following comparisons to see another example of the improvement that hanging punctuation can bring to your presentation.

"Use hanging punctuation
 to set off your quotes."

"if not, the quote gets
lost in the text."

Things to do in Paris:

• Visit The Tour Eiffel
• Check out the exhibit
at the Museé D'Orsay
• Walk along the banks
of the Seine

Things to do in Paris:

• Visit The Tour Eiffel
• Check out the exhibit
  at the Museé D'Orsay
• Walk along the banks
  of the Seine

UNDERLINING It is never acceptable to underline a bold heading like this:

The reason you bold a headline in the first

<u>don't underline this</u>

place is to attract attention to that word or section. It's not necessary to also underline it. Bolding is always preferable to underlining. Especially when underlined text represents a hyperlink when it's used on the Web.

REVERSED TEXT Reversed text is white (or light) text on a dark background. This doesn't work for large blocks of text as you can see from the example below.

> Marshall McLuhan theorized that "The medium is the message." proposing that the means used to communicate a message is more important and has more impact than the message itself.

Your primary goal should always be to make your text as easy to read as possible — if, in fact, you want someone to read it.

> **Marshall McLuhan theorized that "The medium is the message." proposing that the means used to communicate a message is more important and has more impact than the message itself.**

In this example, we increased the character spacing, and bolded the typeface. This makes it easier to read and attracts attention to your headline or callout.

LEADING Leading (or line spacing) is the space (measured in points) between rows of text, from baseline to baseline. Points are equal to $1/72$ of an inch. The term "leading" derives from the days when thin strips of lead were placed between metal lines of type to space them apart.

Present your message so that it will not be ignored. Lean and mean...
Kick it out

This is 9-point Trade Gothic Bold, with 12-point leading.

Present your message so that it will not be ignored. Lean and mean...
Kick it out

This is 9-point Trade Gothic Bold, with 9-point leading.

As you can see, your line spacing really makes a difference in the readability of your text.

KERNING Kerning is the process of improving appearance and legibility by adjusting the white space between certain paired characters (kerning pairs). Most type designers create special "kerning pairs" for their font. Some well-known kerning pairs are To, Te, Ta.

To
To
To

Some graphics programs let you adjust these settings to your liking. You can see the difference in the manually adjusted kerning pairs below.

7.27.01
Without kerning

7.27.01
With manually applied kerning

CHARACTER SPACING Be careful with character spacing. There aren't many instances in which adjusting the spacing is useful, especially if you are creating large areas of text. However, in the examples above, you can see how useful spacing can be to emphasize a point. I particularly like to use this method for logo design.

CHARACTER
spacing

CHARACTER
s p a c i n g

DOUBLE SPACES BETWEEN SENTENCES In the "old days," when we had to use typewriters to communicate, the standard practice was to type two spaces after the period at the end of the sentence. Today's typographers have designed smart fonts that automatically provide the appropriate amount of space when you hit the space character. Never use double spaces between your sentences. It's wrong… wrong… wrong.

SMART QUOTATION MARKS VERSUS INCH MARKS It's fairly obvious in the above example, which is better. If you are going to use quotation marks, make sure you use the smart characters. Key combinations you use on a Mac to get smart quotations marks are:

"These are inch marks."

"These are smart quotes."

Shift-Option-}   '

Shift-Option-]   '

Shift-Option-["

Shift-Option-{   "

On a PC, you can choose an option within the word processing program to convert straight quotes to smart quotation marks. (In Word, the option can be found in the AutoCorrect dialog box.)

ORPHANS AND WIDOWS

A widow is a single word that is left over at the end of a column of text: like the last word in this column.

An orphan is the last word in a paragraph that doesn't fit at the bottom of a column and ends up (alone) on the top of the next. Change your letter spacing, or omit words, but always make your text fit into the appropriate space.

EM DASH VERSUS DOUBLE HYPHEN When people used typewriters, they typed two hyphens to indicate missing material or a pause in thought. In the age of desktop typography, this is no longer acceptable. Use the em dash instead. It takes its name from the letter "M" and is the same width as that character (traditionally the M is the widest letter in that typeface).

Whatever you do -- don't use a double hyphen. If you are showing a break in thought — use an em dash.

You can add spaces to either side of the dash or not have space at all. Just make sure, as always, that you set a rule and maintain consistency.

TYPE BOOKS The information in this chapter just skims the surface of the proper use of type. There are many great books to read if you are interested in learning more. These are some of my favorites:

The PC Is Not a Typewriter: A Style Manual for Creating Professional-Level Type on Your Personal Computer by Robin Williams. Peachpit Press. 1992.

Stop Stealing Sheep & Find Out How Type Works by Erik Spiekermann and E.M. Ginger. Adobe Press. 1993.

The Thames and Hudson Manual of Typography by Ruari McLean. Thames and Hudson, Ltd. 1980.

The Art & Technology of Typography by Compugraphic Corporation. 1988.

Digital Type Design Guide; The Page Designer's Guide to Working with Type by Sean Cavanaugh. Hayden Books. 1995.

JOSEPH LOWERY ON WEB LAYOUT

Joseph Lowery is the author of the Dreamweaver Bible *and the* Fireworks Bible *series as well as the* Dreamweaver UltraDev 4 Bible. *His latest book,* From FrontPage to Dreamweaver *includes a CD-ROM training disc. His books are international best sellers, having sold over 200,000 copies worldwide in 9 different languages. Joseph is also a consultant and trainer and has presented at Seybold in both Boston and San Francisco, Macromedia UCON in the U.S. and Europe, and at ThunderLizard's Web World. As a partner in Deva Associates, Ltd., Joseph developed the Deva Tools for Dreamweaver set of navigational extensions.*

THE WEB CAN BE A STRANGE AND ALIEN UNIVERSE especially if you're coming from a print background. This brief primer is aimed at demystifying the Internet for you and designed to give you a sense of where the ever-changing Web is at this point in time. In addition to an overview of how the Internet works, we'll also explore some of the best practices in Web layout and design.

FORMATTING THE WEB Almost all of the current slate of Web authoring tools — including Dreamweaver from Macromedia, GoLive from Adobe, and FrontPage from Microsoft — allow you to lay out your pages with tools somewhat similar to those found in print layout programs. However, if you want to truly take control of your page and avoid constant frustrations, you have to understand the basics of HTML (Hypertext Markup Language), which is the page description language of the World Wide Web. Browsers such as Internet Explorer, Netscape Communicator, and Opera translate the HTML sent by Web servers into visual displays of text, images, and multimedia.

LOOKING AT TAGS AND ATTRIBUTES One of the reasons that the Web grew so quickly is that its underlying structure, HTML, is readily available and relatively easy to understand. You can look at the HTML code (also called the *source* or *page source*) for almost any Web page in your browser by choosing the appropriate View menu command: In Internet Explorer, use View > Source; for Netscape, choose View > Page Source. HTML code is essentially a formatted text file. In other words, the text is "marked up" with special tags enclosed in angle brackets (like <b>) as can be seen in Figure 1.

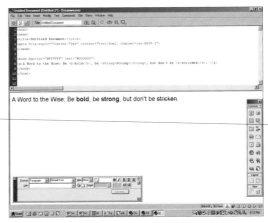

Figure 1. See if you can spot which HTML tags create which text effect.

The code shown in Figure 1 actually represents an entire HTML page. You'll note that there is a tag at the top of the page, <html>, and a similar tag at the bottom of the page, </html>. Together, the opening <html> and the closing </html> denote all that is enclosed as HTML to be rendered by the browser. HTML uses opening and closing tags to surround affected text.

Most tags also have attributes that modify the tag in some way. The <body> tag, for example, which denotes what's in the body of the document (and thus visible), often includes an attribute that specifies the background color, like this:
<body bgcolor="#FFFFFF">

> **NOTE** Because of the large number of RGB color possibilities, HTML colors are specified in hexadecimal (base 16) triplets rather than color names. #FFFFFF translates to Red = 255, Green = 255, Blue = 255 — also known as white.

FORMATTING WEB TEXT Compared to print, typography options on the Web are extremely limited. The basic method of controlling type is by use of the <font> tag. With <font> tag attributes, you can only alter the typeface, size, and color — and each of these attributes has further limitations:

TYPEFACE Browsers use the fonts available on the viewer's computer to render HTML text. Because Web pages are intended for a cross-platform audience, a family of fonts is specified as the typeface value rather than a single font, like this: <font face="Arial, Helvetica, sans serif">. Browsers attempt to use the first member of the font family; if the font is not installed on the viewer's system, the next listed font is used, and so on. The final member of the font family is a generic name (serif, sans serif, cursive, fantasy, or monospace) understood by the browser.

SIZE Font size is specified as one of seven relative values, 1–7, where 1 is the smallest size and 7 is the largest as shown in the font chart in Figure 2. (Just to keep you on your toes, you'll note that this is opposite from the way standard heading sizes are displayed.) The final rendered size depends on the browser and user settings. Relative sizes are used in HTML, rather than the specific point sizes familiar to print-oriented designers.

Figure 2. HTML font sizes are relative to each other and may not always be displayed in the shown point sizes — that's up to the browser and the user settings.

ESSENTIAL HTML TAGS There are well over a hundred HTML tags, but the vast majority of pages use only a handful of key tags. The following table details the essential tags for a basic page:

TAG	DESCRIPTION
<html>... </html>	Defines what's in an HTML page; browsers ignore code, notably server-side code, placed outside these tags.
<head>... </head>	Contains information relating to the entire page, such as its title and indexing information for search engines. You'll also find JavaScript functions, discussed in the Web Languages chapter, and Cascading Style Sheet declarations (explained later in this chapter) within the <head> tags.
<title>... </title>	Holds the title of the page displayed in the browser's title bar. More importantly, a Web page's title is a key element used by search engines for indexing a document.
<meta>... </meta>	Stores general information about the page, most notably its description (in a sentence format) and keywords (in a list format). Search engines also use the description and keywords for indexing pages.
<body>... </body>	Encloses all the visual elements of a page, separate from the <head> tags.
<h1>... </h1>, <h2>... </h2>, etc. through <h6>... </h6>	Converts enclosed text into a heading of a particular size. The heading sizes <h1> through <h6> are relative to one another with <h1> being the largest. The actual displayed size depends on the browser and user settings, with <h1> roughly comparable to 36-pt type and <h6> to 8-pt type.
<p>... </p>	Formats contained text as a paragraph. Each paragraph is separated by a line return; paragraphs may be aligned left, right, or center in HTML.
<img>	Gives the location and attributes for an image file, inserted into an HTML page. Note that <img> does not have a closing tag; all necessary attributes — such as the source path (src), height, and width — are contained within the single tag.
<a href>... </a>	Sets the enclosed text or image as a hyperlink to another page on the Web. The <a> tag, known as the *anchor* tag, is what makes the Web the Web — by providing interconnections from one page and/or site to another.

COLOR For years, standard Web practice has been to use only one of the 216 Web-safe colors for text. Web-safe colors are those common to the major browsers; every major Web authoring tool allows the easy selection of these colors. Recently, designers recognizing that the overwhelming majority of Web surfers use systems that are capable of displaying thousands of colors, designers are beginning to use colors outside the Web-safe range. As noted earlier, colors are specified as RGB values in a hexadecimal triplet format.

Obviously, the HTML <font> tag leaves a lot to be desired. Luckily, another method of formatting text — and Web pages in general — has emerged. *Cascading Style Sheets* (CSS) is a wide-ranging specification developed by the World Wide Web Consortium, also known as the *W3C*. With CSS, designers not only can set font size in points (or picas, ems, or pixels, among other measurement methods); they also can determine the line height (leading) of the text as well as use full justification as shown in Figure 3. CSS support, begun with the release of the version 4.0 browsers, has been less than ideal; not all of the CSS specifications were supported by the browsers, and CSS elements varied from browser to browser. However, designers are increasing their use of CSS for basic text formatting. CSS can affect standard HTML tags in a page, such as <p> or <h1>, or can be used to create custom styles that can be applied on a case-by-case basis.

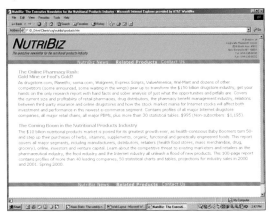

Figure 3. When viewed through a CSS-capable browser, a page using Cascading Style Sheets formatting offers far more typography control than one using regular HTML formatting.

One of the best aspects of CSS is the ability to contain all the formatting information in a style sheet separate from the HTML page. With this ability, designers can link multiple pages in their Web site to the same external style sheet and alter the entire site by modifying the one document. Cascading Style Sheets is slated to become increasingly important for future Web development, and designers should pay close attention to this technology.

> **NOTE** Cascading Style Sheets may also be used for laying out a page, as discussed later in this chapter.

USING GRAPHICS ON THE WEB Two basic formats, GIF and JPEG, account for almost all the imagery you see on the Web. While there are other — often more robust — formats such as PNG, none have the browser support that GIF and JPEG enjoy. Most graphic applications such as Photoshop, Illustrator and Fireworks have options for exporting their files as either GIF or JPEG. Which you choose depends on the characteristics of the image itself.

A GIF file is only capable of displaying a maximum of 256 colors and is best suited for illustrations in which there are large regions of flat color. Many logos are stored as GIFs. The GIF format has two other special characteristics. First, GIFs allow one or more colors to become transparent. GIF transparency is a simple on/off switch; no separate levels of opacity are available. The transparency feature allows GIF images to disguise the rectangular nature of all files, as can be seen in Figure 4. Second, GIFs may be animated through a technique that is similar to flipping pages. Many Web banners are stored as animated GIFS.

The JPEG format was developed by the Joint Photographic Experts Group and, as you might suspect, is used primarily for photographs and other continuous-tone imagery. JPEG graphics are capable of displaying thousands of colors; however, no portion of the image may be transparent or animated.

Often an overall graphic may include some portions that are stored best as a JPEG and others that require GIF features. Such images may be sliced into

Figure 4. Thanks to GIF transparency, the family appears to emerge from the gradient background, and the beanie hat spins with a little help from GIF animation.

separate sections by graphic applications; each section may be saved in a different format as needed. The sliced image is reassembled in the browser as an HTML table that retains the overall look of the entire graphic.

The key concept to keep in mind when developing graphics for the Web is *optimization*. A Web image must be optimized to look as good as possible at the smallest possible file size. (You can use a graphic editor such as Photoshop or Fireworks to optimize JPEG images.) JPEG images use a sliding quality scale to reduce file size; the lower the quality setting, the less sharp the graphic will appear. However, because of the relatively low resolution of the screen — 72 dpi (dots per inch) as opposed to 9600 dpi or higher for print — many graphics don't start to degrade noticeably until they reach the 50% quality setting, as can be seen in Figure 5.

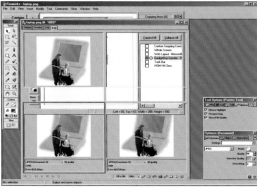

Figure 5. Macromedia's Fireworks shows views of the same file with different JPEG settings to help with optimization choices.

To reduce the file size of a GIF image, the number of colors is reduced. Not all illustrations require 256 colors; if a file looks the same with 128 colors, the file size can typically be cut in half.

Image files are stored separately from the HTML file they belong to, either in the same folder or in their own nearby folder. It's a good idea to save your source files in a separate folder for future editing. You can also use an image from another folder or from anywhere on the Web by supplying a valid Internet address (URL) to the file.

APPROACHES TO WEB LAYOUT As designed, HTML is basically a top-to-bottom layout. The headings appearing at the top of the code are displayed at the top of the page, followed by the paragraphs or images that are inserted in the code next. Images may appear in line with text or aligned to the right or left of a text block.

To overcome this limitation, designers first turned to HTML tables as layout structures. This technique, described below, is still in wide use today. With the increased proliferation of CSS-capable browsers, designers are beginning to use Cascading Style Sheets for layout; you'll find a discussion of this method later in this chapter.

WORKING WITH TABLE-BASED LAYOUT The <table> tag was originally developed so that tables of data — similar to what you find in a spreadsheet — could be more easily displayed in Web pages. Designers discovered that it could also be used as a formatting skeleton for an entire Web page, where elements such as text and images are placed within table cells so that they can appear at an approximate point on a page. Because of their relative complexity, tables are often created in visual editors, rather than by hand-coding.

The <table> tag always contains two helpers: the <tr> (table row) tag and the <td> (table data) tag. The <tr> tag simply says, "Everything within me is a table row." The <td> tag, which always goes within a <tr> tag, is a table cell. Columns aren't specified; they're implied by the number of cells in a row. An empty table with two rows and three columns would look like this:

```
<table>
<tr> <td></td> <td></td> <td></td> </tr>
<tr> <td></td> <td></td> <td></td> </tr>
</table>
```

Note that the string of three <td></td> pairs in each row implies the columns. If all tables were completely empty, formatting tables by hand would be much simpler, but after you start to fill them with content, they're a little harder to grasp at first glance. Here's the code for a table with a heading in the first row, an empty second row, and a third row with a figure next to a paragraph of text:

```
<table width="500" border="0">
  <tr>
    <td colspan="2"><h1>The Mona Lisa
    Page</h1></td>
  </tr>
  <tr>
    <td> </td>
    <td> </td>
  </tr>
  <tr>
    <td><p><img src="mona.gif"
    width="125" height="160"
    alt="The Mona Lisa by Leonardo
    daVinci"></p></td>
    <td><p><font face="Verdana,
    Helvetica, sans-serif"
    color="FF0000">Perhaps the most famous
    portrait ever painted,
    Leonardo daVinci's Mona Lisa is
    often praised for its depiction
    of her enigmatic style.</font>
    </p>
    </td>
  </tr>
</table>
```

You can see the results in Figure 6. I've turned the borders back on so you can see where the individual table rows and cells are located.

Tables used for layout purposes almost always have their borders set to zero to avoid making the structure obvious. The width of the table is either set to an absolute value given in pixels, or a percentage of the screen size. If the latter technique is used, the table will grow or shrink as the browser window is resized. For complex layouts, it's possible to nest one table inside another and have the nested table set to 100% within a set pixel width of the outer table.

The Mona Lisa Page

Perhaps the most famous portrait ever painted, Leonardo daVinci's Mona Lisa is often praised for its depiction of her enigmatic style.

Figure 6. Tables are often used to simulate magazine type layouts with a headline, figure, and text.

CASCADING STYLE SHEETS LAYOUT For all the sophistication designers have been able to wring out of table layouts, the truth is that tables really weren't meant for layout. Cascading Style Sheets, however, were developed with layout in mind. With CSS, you can precisely position any HTML element — whether it's a block of text, an image, or any multimedia object — anywhere on the page. Thus, in theory at least, CSS is far easier to use than tables for layout.

The key tool in CSS layout is the *division* or <div> tag; the <div> tag is commonly called a *layer*. Layers are essentially bounding boxes positioned relative to the upper-left corner of the page; layers may also be nested and placed relative to the outer layer, as seen in Figure 7. In addition to pixel-precise placement, layers may appear in front of or behind other layers. This illusion of depth is controlled by a layer's z-index property.

So, if layers are so great, why doesn't everyone use them for layout? Again, it's a matter of browser support. Only version 4.0 browsers and above can render layers at all, and only the most recent browsers (Internet Explorer 5 and Netscape 6) offer robust support. However, the benefits of using CSS for layout are so impressive that designers encourage their use wherever possible.

The Web can be surprisingly cross-platform when you consider that Netscape browsers act similarly on Windows, Macintosh, and Linux, but you need to keep a few major caveats in mind if you want your Web pages to look similar on those different platforms.

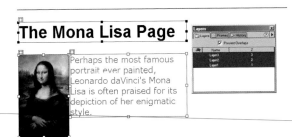

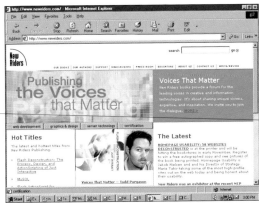

The Mona Lisa Page

Perhaps the most famous portrait ever painted, Leonardo daVinci's Mona Lisa is often praised for its depiction of her enigmatic style.

Figure 7. To lay out the same basic page with layers requires three layers individually positioned.

COLOR Graphics developed on a Macintosh appear darker when displayed on a PC; likewise PC images appear lighter on a Macintosh. This phenomenon is caused by a different gamma value used for each operating system. Many graphic applications offer commands to allow you to view an image under different gamma conditions. As with file size, the key here is to produce the optimum image, one that looks best on both computer systems.

FONTS Before the Web existed, computer-based publishing was primarily print publishing. Therefore, choosing a font in a computer program has traditionally meant choosing a point size. Displaying a 12-pt font on a pixel-based computer display requires that the computer convert points, which are $1/72$ of an inch, into pixels (px), the smallest dots a computer monitor can display.

A Web page displayed on a Macintosh, where the font is specified as 10-pt is displayed as expected because the Mac uses the standard 72 dpi. The same Web page on a Windows computer shows the specified 10-pt font as a 12-pixel font because Windows utilizes 96 dpi as a base scale, as shown in Figures 8 and 9. Font sizes are approximately 25% larger on a PC than on a Macintosh. One workaround used by some designers is to format their pages with CSS; this works only if a pixel measurement scale is used rather than points, ems or any other method.

Figures 8 and 9. Which of these two views of the New Riders site was captured on Mac? If you chose the one on the bottom, you're right! The one on the top was captured on a PC. See the difference?

FORM WIDGETS are provided by a computer's operating system, not by the browser, so they look different on each platform and are often differently sized. For example, a text field set to size="25" will be larger on the PC than on the Macintosh. Web authors need to be aware of these differences and allow for it in their designs, leaving extra space as necessary and testing on other platforms whenever possible. One common mistake is to mix form widgets with image buttons that look like the form widgets on your particular operating system. Mac OS X-form widgets are especially different from those on other operating systems — they look like translucent glass — and can really change the look of your page.

EXAMINING THE BROWSERS Different projects may require you to target different audiences with different types of browsers. For example, if you're authoring a site that provides tips for using Windows 2000, you can expect the overwhelming majority of your audience to be using Internet Explorer 5 running on Windows 2000, because Internet Explorer 5 is included with Windows 2000. An online magazine for Web professionals might have an audience that's using very current versions of Internet Explorer or Navigator running on both Windows and Macintosh. A general shopping site will probably target just about anybody, including users of multiple versions of Macintosh, Windows, and AOL browsers. Being familiar with the capabilities and quirks of the browsers you're targeting and — as always — testing, testing, testing will avoid ugly surprises later.

NETSCAPE NAVIGATOR (COMMUNICATOR) Navigator 1, 2, and 3 are virtually nonexistent now, but Navigator 3 is a good browser to target and test with if you plan to build a site for a wide audience. It was the first "mature" browser, gaining a wide audience, and its feature set was mimicked by browsers that came later. For the most part, if your page works well in Navigator 3, it may not need more than a little tweaking to look very much the same in later versions of Navigator, in Internet Explorer, or in other browsers such as Opera.

Although Navigator 4.x has dwindled in popularity during the wait for the next version of Navigator, it remains the most popular non-Microsoft browser, and the trickiest to develop for. It supports some CSS features, including layers, but not to W3C standards. It contains a widely known bug that causes it not to reload a page without CSS formatting if the user resizes the browser window. Navigator 4.x is available for Windows, Macintosh, OS/2, Linux, and many, many other UNIX platforms. Keep in mind that browser plug-ins are platform-dependent, and most exist only in

Windows and Macintosh versions. When combined with a complete Internet suite, it's called *Netscape Communicator*, but the browser component is still the same.

Netscape's long-awaited update to Navigator 4 is Navigator 6, a completely new product based on the Open Source work of the Mozilla.org team. Netscape 6 provides excellent support for HTML 4 and CSS 1 standards, but has received only lukewarm product reviews. The Open Source status of the major components of Netscape 6 suggests that the HTML rendering engine — called *Gecko* — will likely be built into a range of software and hardware products such as other Web browsers or set-top boxes. Web professionals should definitely keep an eye on these developments, particularly now that America Online owns Netscape.

MICROSOFT INTERNET EXPLORER Internet Explorer 1 and 2 were very limited in their feature sets, not widely used, and can be ignored completely. Internet Explorer 3 includes some basic CSS features, but they are implemented poorly and in a completely different way than Internet Explorer 4, so targeting CSS at Internet Explorer 3 is not recommended. The JavaScript engine built into the Windows version of Internet Explorer 3 doesn't support image swaps — used to create rollover buttons — and the effect is not displayed.

Internet Explorer 4 for Windows generally renders HTML pages very well and supports — albeit incompletely — a number of advanced Web technologies. Its reputation is marred by its forced integration with Windows and its refusal to play nice with a Netscape browser installed on the same machine. Internet Explorer 5 for Windows improved standards support, but many Web developers still target the feature set of Internet Explorer 4 (although testing in Internet Explorer 5 is recommended). Internet Explorer 5.5 for Windows introduced a new range of Microsoft-specific HTML extensions, recalling the bad old days when browser manufacturers competed mainly in new ways to encourage Web developers to create pages that would work only in one brand of browser.

Internet Explorer for Macintosh is an entirely different animal from the Windows versions, with different development teams, codebases, and rendering engines. Internet Explorer 3 and 4 for Macintosh have pretty user interfaces, but are frankly lousy browsers. However, Internet Explorer 5 for Macintosh is a completely different story. It continues the Macintosh Internet Explorer tradition of an excellent user interface and adds one of the most standards-compliant rendering engines of any shipping browser.

As far as plug-in and scripting support in Internet Explorer, the Windows and Macintosh versions are entirely different as well. Internet Explorer for Windows uses Windows-only technologies such as ActiveX and VBScript, although it has basic support for Netscape plug-ins and excellent JavaScript support as well. The Mac version uses Netscape plug-ins and JavaScript exclusively, although its support for both in versions 3 and 4 is the worst of any major browser. The support for plug-ins and JavaScript in Internet Explorer 5 for Macintosh is excellent. Remember that browser plug-ins are platform-dependent, although Macintosh versions of all major plug-ins are available.

AMERICA ONLINE AOL 3, 4, and 5 browsers are modified versions of Microsoft's Internet Explorer, but, unfortunately, the version numbers do not always correspond. In other words, an AOL 4 browser may be based on Internet Explorer 3 or Internet Explorer 4. The major modification to keep in mind is that AOL browsers use a single-window — they do not allow a second window to be opened. AOL caches and recompresses images, which can cause artifacts to appear in some JPEGs. Images are also limited to 640 x 480 in size. For more about authoring for AOL, see AOL's Webmaster page at http://Webmaster.aol.com.

JOSEPH LOWERY ON WEB LANGUAGES

Joseph Lowery is the author of the Dreamweaver Bible *and the* Fireworks Bible *series as well as the* Dreamweaver UltraDev 4 Bible. *His latest book,* From FrontPage to Dreamweaver *includes a CD-ROM training disc. His books are international best sellers, having sold over 200,000 copies worldwide in 9 different languages. Joseph is also a consultant and trainer and has presented at Seybold in both Boston and San Francisco, Macromedia UCON in the U.S. and Europe, and at ThunderLizard's Web World. As a partner in Deva Associates, Ltd., Joseph developed the Deva Tools for Dreamweaver set of navigational extensions.*

IN THE BEGINNING, the Web was HTML, pure and simple. To take full advantage of the Internet's Hypertext protocol — the http:// at the start of all Web addresses — mixing text, graphics and links, you had to use Hypertext Markup Language. Today, however, the Web entertains as many languages as the Tower of Babel, although with slightly better translation.

HTML was never a sitting target. From its very inception, the language was always being modified and enhanced to better fit the growing needs and capabilities of the Internet. The primary keepers of the language, the World Wide Web Consortium (W3C), is a blend of developers and designers from both the private and public sectors. Their goal is to propose and certify language standards that may or may not be adopted in the real world of browsers and Internet devices.

Strictly speaking, the last version of pure HTML was initially released in 1997 with HTML 4.0. The major browsers (Internet Explorer, Netscape Navigator, and Opera) have implemented the vast majority of the W3C's 4.0 recommendations. A minor revision of the language, version 4.01, was put forth in late 1999 (see http://www.w3.org/TR/1999/REC-html401-19991224/). However, the W3C have announced that no further versions of HTML, as such, will be developed.

This does not mean that the primary language of the Web has stopped growing. On the contrary, a major revision of the language has been formulated: XHTML. Before exploring this latest incarnation of HTML, you'll need to have a grasp of another language, *XML*.

XML is short for Extensible Markup Language and, as the name implies, is a completely customizable language. Like HTML, tags are used to mark up text; unlike HTML, the tags are contextual and vary from application to application. For example, let's say that you were working on a site for a car dealership. A sample line of text might be coded in XML like this:

The <car manufacturer="Ford" type="Minivan">Voyager</car> is now available for <msrp>$16,000</msrp>.

Because the text is marked according to its content rather than its appearance, the "look" can change according to the device reading the page. So, on the Web, the price of the car, marked by the <msrp> tag, may be in bold and italic, while the same output could be uppercased on a Web phone. XML offers much greater flexibility than HTML and is rapidly being adopted by industries for many business-to-business applications.

The next incarnation of HTML is known as *XHTML*. In essence, the W3C decided to embrace the more refined structure of XML without totally foregoing the legacy of HTML. XHTML retains almost all the tags of HTML in a slightly different syntax. In XHTML, for instance, all tags must be closed in one way or another. If the tag begins to enclose content, like a <p> (paragraph) tag, it must have a matching closing tag, </p>. If the tag does not enclose any elements, like the line break tag, the closing slash is within the tag itself: the HTML line break tag, <br>, becomes <br/> in XHTML.

Although XHTML doesn't have widespread browser support at the moment, the language is gaining momentum very quickly. Intranets, especially, are beginning to incorporate XHTML as they seek ways to enhance the flow of information without increasing the workload.

JAVASCRIPT, JSCRIPT, AND VBSCRIPT HTML is really good at presenting simple pages on a variety of platforms, but as for making Web pages act like computer applications, forget it. To achieve any degree of interactivity — whether it's a button changing its look during a rollover or a page opening in another browser window — another language must be used in conjunction with HTML. Although there are several contenders to the interactive throne, including VBScript and JScript, the hands-down winner is JavaScript.

The first point that needs to be made about JavaScript is that it's not *Java*. Java is Sun Microsystem's cross-platform compiled language for Web and non-Web applications. The development of Java elements on the Web, called *applets*, requires understanding an altogether different computer language, similar to the C programming language. On the other hand, JavaScript, like HTML, is a scripting language, and while not as easy to grasp as HTML is far easier to use than Java.

Most of the Web authoring tools on the market today use JavaScript to create their special effects. For many developers, no further knowledge of JavaScript is required. However, if you want to include some custom interactions, many of them can be created with JavaScript because it gives you a great deal of control over the browser window and HTML form elements.

Many of the cutting-edge features seen on the Web today are created with a combination of JavaScript and Cascading Style Sheets (CSS). With JavaScript and CSS you can accomplish these tasks:

- Reposition content on a page on the fly.
- Show (or hide) page elements interactively.
- Move animated or static images across the page.
- Make one object appear in front of or behind another object.
- Allow the user to drag an image across the screen and then trigger a response depending on where the graphic is dropped.

To take advantage of the full power of CSS and JavaScript, you'll need to create your pages with the more recent browsers in mind. Browser versions 4.0 and above are required for any sort of CSS/JavaScript work, with an increased number of features available for more recently released browsers such as Netscape 6 and Internet Explorer 5.5.

SERVER-BASED LANGUAGES Perhaps the biggest growth area in Web languages has been on the server end of the network. Because each server model has its own syntax, format, and even file extension, it's not unusual for a typical Web session to involve filenames ending in .asp, .cfm, .jsp, and a host of others in addition to the more standard .htm or .html.

To understand the importance of server-based languages, it helps to have a firm grasp of how the text files stored on a remote computer become Web pages viewed in your browser. When you click a link or enter an Internet address in your browser, that address is sent across the Web to the computer housing that page. If the page is standard HIML, the Web server sends the file right back. The text instructions for reassembling that page — in other words, the code — arrive first, followed by all the necessary graphics and other files, until your own computer temporarily has a complete copy of all the files necessary to re-create the page.

If the page includes server-based tags, a slightly different process occurs. The Web server takes a look at the name of the requested file. If the filename ends in anything other than .htm or .html — .asp or .cfm, for example — the Web server forwards the request to the appropriate application server. An Active Server Pages-enabled Web server handles all .asp files, while a ColdFusion application server takes care of all .cfm files. The application server goes through the code and runs any server-side scripting. The server-side code outputs HTML, which is integrated into the rest of the page's HTML and then returned to the initial Web server — which in turn sends it back to the requesting browser.

Server-side code is necessary for any sort of database integration, such as found on e-commerce sites and other data-driven sites. You'll also find server-side pages — often called *Web applications* because more than one page is required to fulfill an objective — controlling access to specific Web site areas, conditionally delivering content (members of a site may see one page while nonmembers see another), or keeping track of a visitor's requests. The e-commerce shopping cart is an example of this type of server-side application.

These are the most popular server-side languages and their file extensions:

- Active Server Pages or ASP (.asp file format), a Microsoft technology supported in all of its servers.
- ColdFusion (.cfm and .cfml file formats), a tag-based language, similar to HTML,

developed by Allaire Corporation, which recently merged with Macromedia.
- JavaServer Pages or JSP (.jsp file format), developed by Sun Microsystems. JSP is often used for business to business and other enterprise applications.
- PHP (.php, .php3, and .php4 file formats), a freely distributed Open Source language that resembles ASP. PHP files are often paired with MySQL, a freely distributed database.

NOTE There is a server-side version of HTML that uses the extensions .shtml and .shtm. With .shtml files, the Web server executes instructions in the document — most often integrated in a separate file called a *server-side include* — before passing it back to the browser as plain HTML. These types of files, while good for a few limited features, are not nearly as robust as the other server models discussed in this section.

UNDERSTANDING PROTOCOLS Information travels across the Internet according to the specifications of a protocol suite called *Transmission Control Protocol/Internet Protocol* (TCP/IP). A *protocol suite* is, quite simply, a collection of protocols or agreements on how to do something. TCP/IP contains over a hundred of them, but here we'll look at just ones the most commonly used.

Hypertext Transfer Protocol (HTTP) carries requests for HTML pages from Web browsers to servers and carries HTML pages back from servers to browsers. As you may imagine, this function is fairly common on the World Wide Web. When a browser and server want to talk privately — during an e-commerce transaction, for example — they use the *Hypertext Transfer Protocol Secure protocol* (HTTPS) instead. When a browser is using HTTPS, a closed lock or similar icon is displayed for the user, and information is encrypted before it's sent. All Web browsers support HTTP; most support HTTPS. An HTTP URL is written http://www.opensrs.com. An HTTPS URL is similar, except it uses an https:// prefix.

File Transfer Protocol (FTP) allows for the copying of files between computers, even different kinds of computers, and for basic file-manipulation functions such as listing a folder of files on a remote computer. Browsers support rudimentary FTP, but a dedicated FTP client such as WS_FTP for Windows or Anarchie or Fetch for Macintosh is needed to take full advantage of the control that FTP allows. Many FTP servers allow anonymous guest logins, where your email address is your password and you have limited privileges. FTP URLs look like this: ftp://ftp.panic.com.

> **TIP** It may seem as though ftp is specified twice in the URL ftp://ftp.panic.com, but that is not the case. The first ftp is the protocol, and the second ftp is the name of the panic.com FTP server. In the same way, HTTP servers are often named www, as in http://www.panic.com.

Simple Mail Transfer Protocol (SMTP) allows different computers on a network to route email to each other. *Post Office Protocol* (POP) is a newer method for receiving mail. Email clients such as Netscape Messenger and Microsoft Outlook Express use SMTP and POP to send and receive email.

Network News Transfer Protocol (NNTP) is used by Internet newsreaders to query news servers and by news servers to deliver news messages. NNTP is responsible for the Usenet news we all know and love. An NNTP URL looks like this: news://forums.macromedia.com/macromedia.fireworks.

NOTE Other protocols use prefixes that are the same as their names (ftp:// for FTP, for example) but NNTP URLs use the news:// prefix.

Real-Time Streaming Protocol (RTSP) is perhaps the sexiest Internet protocol, allowing for the efficient transfer of streaming multimedia files such as audio or video over the Internet. The term *real-time* refers to the fact that audio and video files need to get to the client in a timely fashion so as not to interrupt the presentation. Server software such as QuickTime Streaming Server or RealServer uses RTSP to send information to the QuickTime Player or RealPlayer, respectively. An RTSP URL starts with an rtsp:// prefix. QuickTime Player and RealPlayer both use RTSP to receive streaming multimedia over the Internet.

While the modern Web designer doesn't necessarily have to be fluent in all the languages in use on the Internet, it certainly helps to have a broad understanding of what's out there. In this chapter, I gave an overview of the various Web languages and how they are generally used; for details on how to use HTML, see the Web Layout chapter. If you decide you want to investigate a language further, let me offer one quick note of advice: As with spoken languages, to get the most out of a programming language you have to totally immerse yourself. Just as the best way to learn a foreign tongue is to live in a foreign land, the best way to master a programming language is to design project after project in that language.

JEFF SOUTHARD ON XML

Jeff Southard (pronounced sútherd) began his career in film, but migrated to San Francisco for multimedia — the boom and bust before the dot-coms — to pioneer New Media design and development. His work has garnered many awards, including an Invision Award (Gold for Creative and Technical Excellence) and Shocked Site of the Year (Macromedia), and been featured in publications such as Communication Arts, New Media, and Advertising Age.

As founder and creative director of 415 Inc., Jeff led the design of projects for Apple Computer, Fox Television, Palm Computing, and others. At Xronos, Jeff produced innovative multimedia projects for clients including Chiat/Day Advertising, Macromedia, and Intel. Earlier in his career, Jeff ran a nonprofit television network for college students. He studied at Brown University and the Rhode Island School of Design. His critically acclaimed short film, "Image," screened throughout the country.

As comfortable writing content as code, Jeff understands the limits of digital media and knows how to push them. Recent assignments have taken him deep into interface design and XML-based technologies, a newfound specialty. Today he leads a team designing and developing Web sites and applications — from Flash games to browser-based content management systems. His portfolio and experiments can be found at http://www.jeffsouthard.com.

BUILDING WITH TREES Common wisdom tells us to not "miss the forest for the trees." This advice applies well to conceptualizing projects; you need a clear sense of the big picture before dropping into the details. But when we design and build something as technologically complex as a Web site, we can't miss the forest *or* the trees. As Web designers, we need to understand the underlying technologies we use in order to make the best sites possible. Luckily, as with many things that appear at first to be complex, many of these technologies can be easily understood given the right framework.

```
<html>
  <body>
    <h1>The Elements</h1>
    <table border="1">
      <tr>
        <td>Earth</td>
        <td>Air</td>
      </tr>
      <tr>
        <td>Fire</td>
        <td>Water</td>
      </tr>
    </table>
    <p>Aether too!</p>
  </body>
</html>
```

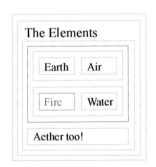

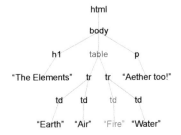

SEE THE TREES In our field, content, code, and design can all be thought of as trees. Programmers use "object hierarchies" to organize their code, while designers organize their drawings into groups, layers, and symbols. Probably the most familiar tree structure is HTML. The figure at left presents a simple HTML document shown in three ways: as indented text you might edit, as nested regions the browser displays, and as a tree diagram. I've highlighted the same two elements in each view.

XML: A TREE OF YOUR OWN DESIGN Once you recognize the familiar HTML tree structure, Extensible Markup Language (XML) becomes considerably less daunting. An XML document is nothing but a tagged text file that defines a tree of elements. Each element can have attributes and can contain text and other child elements, as shown in this example:

```
<elementName
attributeName="attributeValue">
  <childElementName>
...
  </childElementName>
</elementName>
```

The syntax is like the syntax of HTML except that with XML you determine the elements' names and how they will be structured.

But that's just the beginning of the benefits of XML. Using it, you can represent not just Web pages (such as using XHTML) but anything that can be organized as a tree. This includes site maps, page layouts, database content, and even graphics.

Take this hypothetical publishing solution: LifeGuide, a fictional service that promises to "run your life right," has just launched and needs more than a one-off brochure site. They need a complete publishing solution that does all of the following:

- Automates production of a Web site targeting both desktop and handheld computers
- Automates production of print materials such as study guides, self-tests, and fact sheets
- Can be maintained by the LifeGuide staff
- Can be localized in four languages

- Integrates easily with other XML data from content partners

- doesn't use proprietary tools or closed standards.

No problem. We have the right skills and technology for the job. There are many ways in which XML technologies can meet each of these goals; following is a sketch of just one approach to the LifeGuide solution.

DESCRIBING THE SITE CONTENT To start, LifeGuide's site will have about thirty pages in five sections, as shown in this diagram.

Here's how you describe all of the site's content — including the site map — using XML:

```
<site>
   <page><title>Home</title> ... </page>
   <section><title>Overview</title>
      <page><title>How LifeGuide Helps</title>
         <teaser>Your money or your life?</teaser>
         <body>
            <p>Don't leave your life to chance.
               We guarantee that you'll ... </p>
            <p>Take the Self-Test and we'll tell
               you what to do and buy. ... </p>
            ...
         </body>
      </page>
      ...
   </section>
   <section><title>Self-Test</title>
      <question> ... </question>
      ...
   </section>
   <section><title>Results</title> ... </section>
   <section><title>Centers</title> ... </section>
   <section><title>About Us</title> ... </section>
</site>
```

As we move ahead in production, we populate the tree with more detailed content, as we did with this first page of the Overview section.

The Self-Test section of the Web site will gauge visitors' needs through a series of questions. One question asks, "What is your next car going to be?" and presents two options, a sports car or a minivan.

In XML, this question can be represented as follows:

```
<question>
    <text>What is your next car going to be?</text>
    <choice>
        <title>Sports car</title>
        <pro>Makes you feel young.</pro>
        <con>Makes you look adolescent.</con>
        <visual ref="sportsCar" color="red"/>
    </choice>
    <choice>
        <title>Minivan</title>
        <pro>Great for carpooling kids.</pro>
        <con>Carpooling kids.</con>
        <visual ref="minivan" color="green"/>
    </choice>
</question>
```

TRANSFORMING CONTENT INTO WEB PAGES The XML content is then "transformed" into HTML or XHTML (the next, XML-compliant version of HTML) using *Extensible Stylesheet Language Transformations* (XSLT). Below are four sample templates that transform the "question" XML element into HTML. For each <question>, the output tree contains a <div> with the contents of the <text> followed by a <table> and a <tr> of the output of the "choice" template. In turn, the choice template calls the "visual" and "pro/con" templates.

```
<xsl:stylesheet version="1.0"... >
    ...
<xsl:template match="question">
    <div class="titleBlock">
        <xsl:apply-templates select="text"/>
    </div>
    <table cellspacing="10">
        <tr>
            <xsl:apply-templates select="choice"/>
        </tr>
    </table>
</xsl:template>

<xsl:template match="choice">
    <td valign="top">
        <a href="javascript:option({position()})">
            <xsl:apply-templates select="visual"/>
            <div class="titleBlock">
                <xsl:apply-templates select="title"/>
            </div>
        </a>
        <xsl:apply-templates select="prolcon"/>
    </td>
</xsl:template>

<xsl:template match="visual">
    <img src="art/med/{@ref}.gif"
        height="120" border="0"/>
</xsl:template>

<xsl:template match="prolcon">
    <div class="listItem">
        <xsl:value-of select="name()"/>
        <xsl:apply-templates/>
    </div>
</xsl:template>

</xsl:stylesheet>
```

In this way, the templates describe how all the content should be organized and formatted: from sub-page templates like those above to others that describe a whole page with navigation elements.

Naturally, there's a great deal to XSLT, but here is a basic overview:

- XSLT is used to convert one type of XML file into another, such as XHTML. In the process, it can apply formatting, perform calculations, and reorganize the content. The last two features make it more powerful than Cascading Style Sheets (CSS).
- XSLT stylesheets are written in XML. XSLT commands are nested among the XHTML elements. The xsl: prefix identifies those elements as part of the XSLT "namespace" and guarantees that their element names will not conflict with HTML or other XML tag names.
- A template can define an entire page using a fill-in-the-blanks format similar to ASP, JSP, and PHP, but the real power comes in designing small, reusable templates such as those in this example.
- XSLT is not yet widely supported in browsers. As such, you should use the technology on the server side to generate pages for now.

IN THE PIPELINE The automated site production can best be described as a pipeline of transformations from one XML tree to the next. The Self-Test section, for example, would be stored in an XML document, and the data about LifeGuide's counseling centers would be extracted from a relational database as XML. An XSLT stylesheet then pulls this and other content into the greater site content tree.

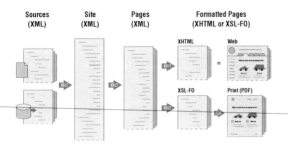

Sources (XML) | Site (XML) | Pages (XML) | Formatted Pages (XHTML or XSL-FO)

Next, XSLT generates all the content for the pages, still without formatting (layout or font size, for example). The final transformation generates the XHTML or HTML pages to be cached and downloaded.

A parallel process generates updated print materials. Pages from the Self-Test section are transformed (using another set of XSLT stylesheets) into an *XSL Formatting Objects* (XSL-FO) document, which is then converted by an XSL processor (such as Apache's FOP) into printable PDF files. Et voilá! — you've covered the print materials base for your client.

Another World Wide Web Consortium (W3C) standard, XSL-FO describes the detailed presentation of documents, much like HTML. But XSL-FO can be controlled as precisely as necessary for digital printing. Think of it as an XML-based version of PDF. Today, there are many tools (such as Apache's Open Source FOP) that convert XSL-FO and Scalable Vector Graphics (SVG) documents into PDF files. I'll explain SVG later.

BRINGING IT ALL TOGETHER The LifeGuide staff will maintain the site themselves. With our XML-based approach, content is separate and the client can easily edit the site without understanding the details of its technical design. Besides letting clients maintain their own content, separating design, content, and code has two big benefits for the production team:

- Different members of the production team can work independently, both in creating and maintaining the site. Designers can update XSLT and image files affecting the look without breaking the programmer's code and vice versa.
- Well-designed templates and code modules can be reused across the project and in future projects.

Here's a representation of this separation and the build engine that brings it all together.

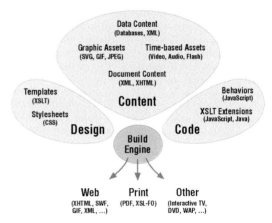

The build engine, as seen in the diagram above, triggers the transformation of raw source files (design, content, and code) into the final output as either a collection of nested folders and files of XHTML, Flash movies, images, and so on for a Web site, or as a set of PDF files for print output.

The build engine can be a simple batch command generated by XSLT from the site tree, a complex Java application, or anything in between.

With some complex coding, this approach can be applied to a dynamic Web site. The site tree would then specify how frequently each part of the site needs to be updated, and the engine would handle the rebuilding and caching of those sections. Some sections might be updated only when the client chooses to do so, while others could update themselves constantly and automatically.

CONTENT MANAGEMENT My favorite aspect of storing content in XML is that we can give our clients an off-the-shelf XML editor to revise content, eliminating the need to build a custom content editor. We simply write a *schema* and let the clients edit the XML themselves. Because XML editors validate content and provide pull-down value lists to aid authors, the quality of the client's work, no matter how novice, is ensured.

An XML document is said to be *well formed* if it conforms to the basic rules of XML (for example, all elements must have a closing tag and be properly nested). An XML document is *valid* if it obeys the rules of its schema. For example, the XHTML schema dictates, among other things, that XHTML files must have one <html> root element containing a <head> element followed by a <body>. In our example, we define that 1) each <question> must have two or more <choice>, 2) each <choice> contains a <title>, and so on. The two most popular schema syntaxes are *Document Type Definition* (DTD) and the less widely supported but newer and more precise *XML Schema*.

These days, all the proprietary content management and databases used by big business can (or will soon be able to) import and export XML.

Expect the Open Source community to release collaborative authoring solutions based on XML in the near future. Meanwhile, in many cases all that's needed is a set of schemas and a structure of XML documents and other files served up with WebDAV, the open collaborative file-sharing protocol supported by MacOS X and Windows XP.

SCALABLE VECTOR GRAPHICS (SVG) SVG, also an XML-based technology, allows us to use XSLT to generate graphics and animations. The technology is similar to Macromedia's Flash format (SWF) but has many unique features such as these:

- Linking to external graphics (such as GIF, PNG, JPEG, and other SVG files)
- CSS for visual formatting
- Filter effects to create shadows, glows, embossing, etc.

Adobe has a robust SVG viewer; but requiring a 2MB download, it's unlikely that it will reach the level of adoption enjoyed by the ubiquitous Flash plug-in. So until SVG is built into browsers (hopefully we'll see it in the forthcoming versions of Netscape and Internet Explorer), we can't count on users having it installed.

A CAR IS A TREE I'll use the car example to illustrate how SVG describes graphics. Flash users should notice how the <defs> section stores reusable graphics like Flash's Library.

```
<svg width="450" height="150"
xmlns="http://www.w3.org/2000/svg">
<title>Sports Car or Minivan?</title>

<!-- The defs element contains symbol definitions
used below -->
<defs>
    <g id="wheel">
      <circle id="tire" r="20" fill="black"/>
      <circle id="hubCap" r="7" fill="white"/>
    </g>
    <line id="fin" x2="20" y2="-10"
    stroke="black" stroke-width="3"/>
    <g id="bikeRack" stroke="black" stroke-
    width="3">
      <line x2="25"/>
      <line x1="25" x2="25" y2="-10"/>
    </g>
</defs>

<!-- The sportsCar group contains the body, 2
wheels, and a fin -->
<g id="sportsCar" transform="translate(100,100)">
    <polygon points="-90,0 30,-60 100,0" fill="red"/>
    <use xlink:href="#wheel" x="-30"/>
    <use xlink:href="#wheel" x="50"/>
    <use xlink:href="#fin" x="70" y="-25"/>
</g>
<!-- The minivan group contains the body, 2
wheels, and a bike rack -->
<g id="minivan" transform="translate(300,100)">
    <polygon points="-80,0 -30,-80 90,-80
    100,0" fill="green"/>
    <use xlink:href="#wheel" x="-25"/>
    <use xlink:href="#wheel" x="60"/>
    <use xlink:href="#bikeRack" x="95" y="-25"/>
</g>
</svg>
```

A TREE IS A TREE One of the most compelling features of SVG is its XML syntax, allowing the same techniques we use to build XHTML to be applied to SVG. To clearly illustrate this, I wrote some XSLT that generates an SVG-based visualization of an XML document tree as... a tree. Elements are branches. Attributes are leaves. Text nodes are fruit.

From left to right, the trees represent a job posting, the W3C home page in XHTML, and a sales transaction. Notice the details and how easily the different elements of the graphics can be broken down and understood, both independently and as parts creating their respective wholes. The first tree stores all its data in the text nodes (fruit); the soaring trunk of the middle tree represents the <table><tbody><tr> sequence in the main table that is used to split the page into three columns; and the last tree uses mostly attributes (leaves) to store data.

I could have built a Flash movie that uses ActionScript code to draw the trees from an imported XML file, but as SVG these graphics can easily be imported into PDF documents or rendered on the server as bitmaps.

SUMMARY AND SUGGESTIONS I hope I've piqued your interest in XML and its related technologies. I believe these newcomers to our field will soon be indispensable in building flexible and maintainable solutions for our clients. Now is the time to get in on the ground floor, so here are my suggestions:

For designers:

- Build your work as trees with nested objects.
- Use reusable symbols and templates.
- Separate formatting from content using styles and CSS.
- Explore the XML features of the new drawing and site design tools.
- Consider learning XSLT — your billable rate will thank you.

For developers:

- Whenever possible, store content in XML.
- Think in terms of the tree and pipeline design patterns.
- Use XSLT for XML-HTML transformations.
- Read books about the W3C recommendations: XML, XHTML, XML Schema, XSLT, and SVG.

And lastly, a quick site guide to help you learn more about the many technologies I've touched on in this essay:

www.w3.org Detailed technical information about XML, its related technologies, and other Web standards.

www.adobe.com/svg Designer-oriented overview of SVG; home of leading SVG viewer.

www.w3schools.com Tutorials and references for XML, XSLT, XML Schema, and so on.

www.jeffsouthard.com Examples of XML trees and XSLT source code.

STEVE KRUG ON USABILITY

Steve Krug's childhood dream of succeeding Don Herbert (TV's Mr. Wizard) was foiled when Don held onto the job for 40 years. So instead of spending his days explaining scientific principles with mousetraps, ping pong balls, dry ice, and a blowtorch, Steve ended up with the next-best career: usability expert.

Since 1987, he has helped companies large (think Apple, Symantec, AOL, Netscape, and Excite@Home) and small ensure that their software and Web sites are truly easy to use. And since he wrote Don't Make Me Think! A Common Sense Approach to Web Usability (New Riders), *Steve has been busy giving speeches, teaching usability workshops (public and private), and reviewing Web site designs for his clients. His consulting firm, Advanced Common Sense, lives online at http://www.sensible.com.*

This chapter reprinted from Don't Make Me Think! A Common Sense Approach to Web Usability (New Riders) *www.stevekrug.com*

Michael, why are the drapes open?
—Kay Corleone in *The Godfather, Part II*

PEOPLE OFTEN ASK ME "What's the most important thing I should do if I want to make sure my Web site is easy to use?"

The answer is simple. It's not "Nothing important should ever be more than two clicks away," or "Speak the user's language," or even "Be consistent."

It's... **"DON'T MAKE ME THINK!"**

I've been telling people for years that this is my first law of usability. And the more Web pages I look at, the more convinced I become.

It's the overriding principle — the ultimate tie breaker when deciding whether something works or doesn't in a Web design. If you have room in your head for only one usability rule, make this the one.[1]

It means that as far as is humanly possible, when I look at a Web page it should be self-evident. Obvious. Self-explanatory.

I should be able to "get it" — what it is and how to use it — without expending any effort thinking about it.

Just how self-evident are we talking?

Well, self-evident enough, for instance, that your next-door neighbor, who has no interest in the subject of your site and who barely knows how to use the Back button, could look at your site's home page and say, "Oh, it's a _____." (With any luck, she'll say, "Oh, it's a _____. Neat." But that's another subject.)

THINK OF IT THIS WAY When I'm looking at a page that doesn't make me think, all the thought balloons over my head say things like "OK, there's the _____. And that's a _____. And there's the thing that I want."

NOT THINKING

But when I'm looking at a page that makes me think, all the thought balloons over my head have question marks in them.

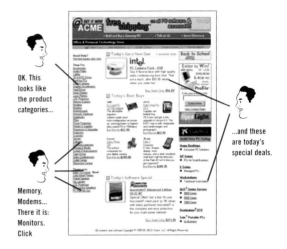

THINKING

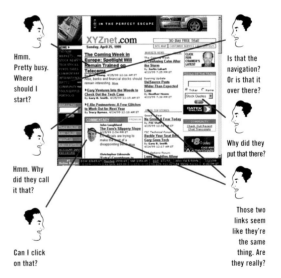

When you're creating a site, your job is to get rid of the question marks.

THINGS THAT MAKE US THINK All kinds of things on a Web page can make us stop and think unnecessarily. Take names of things, for example. Typical culprits are cute or clever names, marketing-induced names, company-specific names, and unfamiliar technical names.

For instance, suppose a friend tells me that XYZ Corp is looking to hire someone with my exact qualifications, so I head off to their Web site. As I scan the page for something to click, the name they've chosen for their job listings section makes a difference.

These things are on a continuum somewhere between "Obvious to everybody" and "Truly obscure," and there are always tradeoffs involved.

OBVIOUS

REQUIRES THOUGHT

For instance, "Jobs" may sound too undignified for XYZ Corp, or they may be locked into "Job-o-Rama" because of some complicated internal politics, or because that's what it's always been called in their company newsletter. My main point is that the tradeoffs should usually be skewed in the direction of "Obvious."

Another needless source of question marks over people's heads are the links and buttons that aren't obviously clickable. As a user, I should never have to devote a millisecond of thought to whether things are clickable—or not.

You may be thinking, "Well, it doesn't take much effort to figure out whether something's click-

able. If you point the cursor at it, it'll change from an arrow to a pointing hand. What's the big deal?"

The point is, when we're using the Web every question mark adds to our cognitive workload, distracting our attention from the task at hand. The distractions may be slight, but they add up. And sometimes it doesn't take much to throw us off.

As a rule, people don't like to puzzle over how to do things. The fact that the people who built the site didn't care enough to make things obvious — and easy — can erode our confidence in the site and its publishers.

Another example: On most bookstore sites, before I search for a book I first have to think about how I want to search.

OBVIOUSLY CLICKABLE

REQUIRES THOUGHT

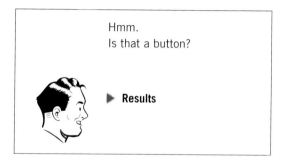

MOST BOOKSTORE SITES

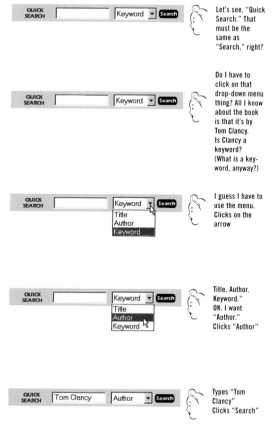

Granted, most of this "mental chatter" takes place in a fraction of a second, but you can see that it's a pretty noisy process. Even something as apparently innocent as jazzing up a well-known name (from "Search" to "Quick Search") can generate another question mark.

Amazon.com, on the other hand, doesn't even mention the Author-Title-Keyword distinction. They just look at what you type and do whatever makes the most sense.

AMAZON.COM

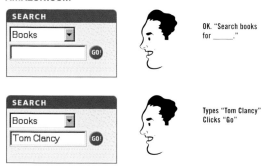

OK. "Search books for _____."

Types "Tom Clancy"
Clicks "Go"

After all, why should I have to think about how I want to search? And even worse, why should I have to think about how the site's search engine wants me to phrase the question, as though it were some ornery troll guarding a bridge? ("You forgot to say 'May I?'")

I could list dozens of other things that visitors to a site shouldn't spend their time thinking about:

- Where am I?
- Where should I begin?
- Where did they put _____?
- What are the most important things on this page?
- Why did they call it that?

But the last thing you need is another checklist to add to your stack of Web design checklists. The most important thing you can do is to just understand the basic principle of eliminating question marks. If you do, you'll begin to notice all the things that make you think while you're using the Web, and eventually you'll learn to recognize and avoid them in the pages you're building.

YOU CAN'T MAKE EVERYTHING SELF-EVIDENT Your goal should be for each page to be self-evident, so that just by looking at it the average user[2] will know what it is and how to use it.

Sometimes, though, particularly if you're doing something original or groundbreaking or something very complicated, you have to settle for self-explanatory. On a self-explanatory page, it takes a little thought to "get it" — but only a little. The appearance of things, their well-chosen names, the layout of the page, and the small amounts of carefully crafted text should all work together to create near-instantaneous recognition.

If you can't make a page self-evident, you at least need to make it self-explanatory.

WHY IS THIS SO IMPORTANT? Oddly enough, not for the reason you usually hear cited:

On the Internet, the competition is always just one click away, so if you frustrate users they'll head somewhere else.

This is sometimes true, but you'd be surprised at how long some people will tough it out at sites that frustrate them. Many people who encounter problems with a site tend to blame themselves and not the site.

The fact is, your site may not have been that easy to find in the first place and visitors may not know of an alternative. The prospect of starting over isn't always that attractive.

And there's also the "I've waited ten minutes for this bus already, so I may as well hang in a little longer" phenomenon. Besides, who's to say that the competition will be any less frustrating?

SO WHY, THEN? Making pages self-evident is like having good lighting in a store: it just makes everything seem better. Using a site that doesn't make us think about unimportant things feels effortless, whereas puzzling over things that don't matter to us tends to sap our energy and enthusiasm — and time.

But the main reason why it's important not to make people think is that they're likely to spend far less time looking at the pages we design than we'd like to think.

As a result, if Web pages are going to be effective, they have to work most of their magic at a glance. And the best way to do this is to create pages that are self-evident, or at least self-explanatory.

Why are things always in the last place you look for them? Because you stop looking when you find them. — Children's riddle

In the past five years I've spent a lot of time watching people use the Web, and the thing that has struck me most is the difference between how we think people use Web sites and how they actually use them.

When we're creating sites, we act as though people are going to pore over each page, reading our finely crafted text, figuring out how we've organized things, and weighing their options before deciding which link to click.

What they actually do most of the time (if we're lucky) is glance at each new page, scan some of the text, and click on the first link that catches their interest or vaguely resembles the thing they're looking for. There are usually large parts of the page that they don't even look at.

We're thinking "great literature" (or at least "product brochure"), while the user's reality is much closer to "billboard going by at 60 miles an hour."

As you might imagine, it's a little more complicated than this, and it depends on the kind of page, what the user is trying to do, how much of a hurry she's in, and so on. But this simplistic view is much closer to reality than most of us imagine.

WHAT WE DESIGN FOR...

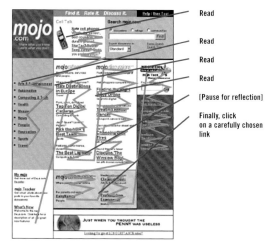

THE REALITY...

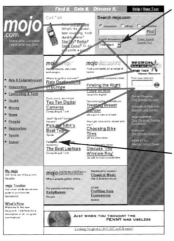

Look around feverishly for anything that
a) is interesting, or vaguely resembles what you're looking for
b) is clickable

As soon as you find a halfway-decent match, click.
If it doesn't pan out, click the Back button and try again.

It makes sense that we picture a more rational, attentive user when we're designing pages. It's only natural to assume that everyone uses the Web the same way we do, and — like everyone else — we tend to think that our own behavior is much more orderly and sensible than it really is.

If you want to design effective Web pages, though, you have to learn to live with three facts about real-world Web use.

FACT OF LIFE #1:
WE DON'T READ PAGES. WE SCAN THEM.

One of the very few well-documented facts about Web use is that people tend to spend very little time reading most Web pages.[3] Instead, we scan (or skim) them, looking for words or phrases that catch our eye.

The exception, of course, is pages that contain documents like news stories, reports, or product descriptions. But even then, if the document is longer than a few paragraphs, we're likely to print it out because it's easier and faster to read on paper than on a screen.

Why do we scan?

- We're usually in a hurry. Much of our Web use is motivated by the desire to save time. As a result, Web users tend to act like sharks: they have to keep moving, or they'll die. We just don't have the time to read any more than necessary.

- We know we don't need to read everything. On most pages, we're really only interested in a fraction of what's on the page. We're just looking for the bits that match our interests or the task at hand, and the rest of it is irrelevant. Scanning is how we find the relevant bits.

- We're good at it. We've been scanning newspapers, magazines, and books all our lives to find the parts we're interested in, and we know that it works.

The net effect is a lot like Gary Larson's classic *Far Side* cartoon about the difference between what we say to dogs and what they hear. In the cartoon, the dog (named Ginger) appears to be listening intently as her owner gives her a serious talking-to about staying out of the garbage. But from the dog's point of view, all he's saying is "blah blah GINGER blah blah blah blah GINGER blah blah blah."

What we see when we look at a Web page depends on what we have in mind, but it's usually just a fraction of what's on the page.

WHAT DESIGNERS BUILD...

WHAT USERS SEE...

I want to buy a ticket.

How do I check my frequent flyer miles?

Like Ginger, we tend to focus on words and phrases that seem to match (a) the task at hand or (b) our current or ongoing personal interests. And of course, (c) the trigger words that are hardwired into our nervous systems like *Free*, *Sale*, *Sex*, and our own names.

FACT OF LIFE #2:
WE DON'T MAKE OPTIMAL CHOICES. WE SATISFICE.

When we're designing pages, we tend to assume that users will scan the page, consider all of the available options, and choose the best one.

In reality, though, most of the time we don't choose the best option—we choose the first reasonable option, a strategy known as *satisficing*.[4] As soon as we find a link that seems like it might lead to what we're looking for, there's a very good chance that we'll click it.

I'd observed this behavior for years, but its significance wasn't really clear to me until I read Gary Klein's book *Sources of Power: How People Make Decisions*.[5] Klein has spent 15 years studying naturalistic decision making: how people such as firefighters, pilots, chessmasters, and nuclear power plant operators make high-stakes decisions in real settings with time pressure, vague goals, limited information, and changing conditions.

Klein's team of observers went into their first study (of field commanders at fire scenes) with the generally accepted model of rational decision making: Faced with a problem, a person gathers information, identifies the possible solutions, and chooses the best one. They started with the hypothesis that because of the high stakes and extreme time pressure, fire captains would be able to compare only two options, an assumption they thought was conservative. As it turned out, the fire commanders didn't compare any options. They took the first reasonable plan that came to mind and did a quick mental test for problems. If they didn't find any, they had their plan of action.

So why don't Web users look for the best choice?

- We're usually in a hurry. And as Klein points out, "Optimizing is hard, and it takes a long time. Satisficing is more efficient."
- There's not much of a penalty for guessing wrong. Unlike firefighting, the penalty for guessing wrong on a Web site is usually only a click or two of the Back button, making satisficing an effective strategy. Of course, this assumes that pages load quickly; when they don't, we have to make our choices more carefully — just one of the many reasons why most Web users don't like slow-loading pages.
- Weighing options may not improve our chances. On poorly designed sites, putting effort into making the best choice doesn't really help. You're usually better off going with your first guess and using the Back button if it doesn't work out.
- Guessing is more fun. It's less work than weighing options, and if you guess right, it's faster. And it introduces an element of chance—the pleasant possibility of running into something surprising and good.

Of course, this is not to say that users never weigh options before they click. It depends on things like their frame of mind, how pressed they are for time, and how much confidence they have in the site.

FACT OF LIFE #3:

WE DON'T FIGURE OUT HOW THINGS WORK. WE MUDDLE THROUGH.

One of the things that becomes obvious as soon as you do any usability testing — whether you're testing Web sites, software, or household appliances — is the extent to which people use things all the time without understanding how they work, or with completely wrong-headed ideas about how they work.

Faced with any sort of technology, very few people take the time to read instructions. Instead,

we forge ahead and muddle through, making up our own vaguely plausible stories about what we're doing and why it works.

It often reminds me of the scene at the end of *The Prince and the Pauper* where the real prince discovers that the lookalike pauper has been using the Great Seal of England as a nutcracker in his absence. (It makes perfect sense — to the pauper, the seal is just this great big, heavy chunk of metal.)

And the fact is, we get things done that way. I've seen lots of people use software and Web sites effectively in ways that are nothing like what the designers intended.

My favorite example is the people (and I've seen at least a dozen of them myself) who will type a site's entire URL in the Yahoo! search box every time they want to go there — not just to find the site for the first time, but every time they want to go there, sometimes several times a day. If you ask them about it, it becomes clear that some of them think that Yahoo is the Internet, and that this is the way you use it.[6]

And muddling through is not limited to beginners. Even technically savvy users often have surprising gaps in their understanding of how things work. (I wouldn't be surprised if even Bill Gates has some bits of technology in his life that he uses by muddling through.)

Most Web designers would be shocked if they knew how many people type URLs in Yahoo!'s search box.

Why does this happen?

- It's not important to us. For most of us, it doesn't matter to us whether we understand how things work as long as we can use them. It's not for lack of intelligence, but for lack of caring. In the great scheme of things, it's just not important to us.

- If we find something that works, we stick to it. Once we find something that works — no matter how badly — we tend not to look for a better way. We'll use a better way if we stumble across one, but we seldom look for one.

It's always interesting to watch Web designers and developers observe their first usability test. The first time they see a user click something completely inappropriate, they're surprised. (For instance, when the user ignores a nice big fat "Software" button in the navigation bar, saying something like, "Well, I'm looking for software, so I guess I'd click here on 'Cheap Stuff' because cheap is always good.") The user may even find what he's looking for eventually, but by then the people watching don't know whether to be happy or not.

The second time it happens, they're yelling "Just click 'Software'!" The third time, you can see them thinking: "Why are we even bothering?"

And it's a good question. If people manage to muddle through so much, does it really matter whether they "get it"? The answer is that it matters a great deal because, while muddling through may work sometimes, it tends to be inefficient and error-prone.

On the other hand, if users "get it":

- There's a much better chance that they'll find what they're looking for, which is good for them and for you.
- There's a better chance that they'll understand the full range of what your site has to offer — not just the parts that they stumble across.
- You have a better chance of steering them to the parts of your site that you want them to see.
- They'll feel smarter and more in control when they're using your site, which will bring them back. You can get away with a site that people muddle through only until someone builds one down the street that makes them feel smart.

IF LIFE GIVES YOU LEMONS... By now you may be thinking (given this less-than-rosy picture of the Web audience and how they use the Web), "Why don't I just get a job at the local 7-11? At least there my efforts might be appreciated."

So, what's a girl to do?

I think the answer is simple: If your audience is going to act like you're designing billboards, then design great billboards.

[1] Actually, there is a close contender: "Get rid of half the words on each page, then get rid of half of what's left."

[2] The actual Average User is kept in a hermetically sealed vault at the International Bureau of Standards in Geneva.

[3] See Jakob Nielson's October 1997 Alertbox column, "How Users Read on the Web" available at www.useit.com.

[4] Economist Herbert Simon coined the term *satisfice* (a cross between satisfy and suffice) in *Models of Man: Social and Rational* (Wiley, 1957).

[5] MIT Press, 1998.

[6] In the same vein, I've encountered many AOL users who clearly think that AOL is the Internet — good news for Yahoo! and AOL.

[7] Web developers often have a particularly hard time understanding — or even believing — that people might feel this way, since they themselves are usually keenly interested in how things work.

SCOTT SMITH ON BROADCAST

Scott Smith's latest film, Carny Tales, *won the Audience Choice Award at the* Sundance Film Festival 2002. *The former publisher of* RES: The Magazine of Digital Filmmaking, *he is a featured columnist on the* Adobe.com *Web site, and the author of several books on moviemaking, including* The Film 100: A Ranking of the Most Influential People in the History of the Movies (Citadel Press), Making iMovies (Peachpit Press), *and the recent* Firewire Filmmaking (Peachpit Press).

CREATING IMAGES FOR TELEVISION: A FEW TIPS ON PREPARING ARTWORK FOR BROADCAST I'm often asked to speculate from which field of the arts the next generation of digital moviemakers will emerge. Will they be sculptors and painters who have tossed aside their chisels and brushes for lightweight handheld camcorders? Will they be frustrated novelists or commercial illustrators eager to see their inanimate words and pictures come to life in progressive frames of video? Will they be the graduates of film schools, looking to break into Hollywood with a low-budget DV project that may eventually lead to a celluloid spectacle they hope to shoot on 70mm Technicolor stock?

No, I always reply, it's more likely the new storytellers will be artists with a background in desktop publishing.

Desktop publishing? How can anyone from the print world succeed in producing television commercials, training videos, short subject documentaries, or independent feature films? In my opinion, these individuals are the best candidates for two reasons. First, they are excellent communicators, experts at telling dramatic stories in short form. Many art directors, after mastering the ability to communicate with quick headlines and colorful design, took these lessons one step further when the Internet rolled around, adapting their publishing savvy to online destinations. Initially, they explored simple enhancements like image maps and animated GIFs to add motion and interactivity to stolid pages, but gradually they reinvented the publishing world by including complex navigation, movement, and sound — through Java and Flash applications. Many of today's best mixed-media Web sites have more action, more clarity, more intrigue — in short, a more compelling "experience" — than most movies ever achieve.

More importantly, graphic designers who cut their teeth in the era of desktop publishing understand the concept of the *digital island*, a self-contained workstation composed of every tool necessary to get the job done. These people embrace do-it-yourself processes, low-cost equipment, and off-the-shelf software. They are skilled at using multiple applications and utilities to tackle a dynamic range of disparate tasks. Forced to work alone or in small groups, usually on the fringes of a large organization, these islanders seek out solutions that keep their media files in an all-digital environment at all times. They are also used to sharing their work with other digital artists (over local networks, removable media, or the Web), so they are best equipped for collaborations when the need arises. These attributes are essential to success in the future of filmmaking.

Still, there are some peculiarities in the video world that intimidate even the most experienced digital creators. Dizzy from the jargon and myth of analog devices, they have stayed away from broadcast design projects. But the desktop video revolution is much like the desktop publishing revolution: both have removed the cumbersome, old-technology rigmarole by offering simpler, streamlined methods. If you're a graphic artist with even the slightest amount of experience in creating animations for the Web, you should no longer fear the moviemaking process. It's really quite easy. Following are a few simple tips to help you produce quality work for television.

USE A REFERENCE MONITOR Just as CMYK images and Pantone inks cannot be accurately reflected on a computer monitor, video images will not display on your monitor as they will on a television set. What's needed is an *NTSC-quality reference monitor* (also called a *production monitor* or *broadcast monitor*) to test the color and clarity of your images. It's such an essential piece of equipment for outputting to broadcast media that it should become part of every desktop video system. Most models around $1,500, like the industry staple 14-inch Sony PVM14M4U Presentation Monitor, are more than adequate for homes or small studios. If you live anywhere in North America, your television complies with the guidelines of the National Television Standards Committee (NTSC), so using a monitor calibrated to the precise NTSC specifications will ensure that your work will display properly on TV sets across the country. Europe and other countries have different standards (PAL, SECAM) for television broadcasting.

Unlike the TV set in your living room, a reference monitor is a calibrated CRT that can show you accurate video signal. Other video devices are prone to drift out of adjustment, but a reference monitor displays the proper ranges of color and luminance for broadcast TV and reveals hidden parts of the image. For digital filmmakers, especially those creating motion graphics from scratch in Adobe Photoshop or Illustrator, the reference monitor is your best chance to see what the final product will look like in the analog realm. After all, nearly all television sets are still analog devices conforming to the broadcasting standards of a particular country; if you are creating movies for broadcast in the United States, you should use an NTSC reference monitor. PAL monitors are the standard for Europe.

Unless you never intend your video project to be shown on TV (let's say it's a streaming file exclusively for the Web or a CD-ROM based training video), you should give serious consideration to making a reference monitor a permanent addition to your production environment. There are some things to look for when purchasing a reference monitor. Avoid models of less than 13 inches (monitors are measured in diagonal inches, from the farthest corners of the cathode-ray tube), because small tubes struggle to represent the flaws in details that may become obvious on larger sets. There's no need to get a huge screen, as the distance between you and the monitor will not be significant. Reference monitors between 13 and 20 inches are the most popular.

Avoid placing the monitor in a workspace prone to unwanted glare or reflections or near electromagnetic equipment that may interfere with the video signal, causing colors to shift, producing ghosted images or wavy lines on the screen. If this interference is unavoidable, consider a monitor with a metal cabinet to shield the signals. Most monitors include a degauss button that will demagnetize the screen; others automatically degauss every time they are turned on.

Typically, you'd also have to purchase a video card for your computer, which sends the digital data from your application to the NTSC monitor. But fortunately, today's reference monitors not only accept professional component connections but also include the S-video and composite analog jacks that are common to home video equipment. This means that if you have a Firewire-enabled computer and a DV camcorder, you can easily connect and convert digital video images into composite analog signals. You simply use the DV camcorder as a go-between, taking pass-through playback from the computer, routing it through Firewire to the camcorder, and then out through the AV adapter cable to your reference monitor.

Several utilities are available that let you use this unique ability to test much more than video playback. EchoFire software from Synthetic Aperture, a simple control panel application, uses the Firewire port to send still images from Adobe Photoshop and After Effects directly to the camcorder, allowing preview of artwork on any analog devices (like a TV set or reference monitor) connected to your camera. Even if your RAM previews inside After Effects are set to display low-resolution feedback to the computer screen, EchoFire will send a full-quality rendered image to the Firewire port. In addition to routing images to the camcorder, EchoFire can instantly stretch the aspect ratio of video to fit the screen or deinterlace still photos so they don't flicker when displayed on a television set. This utility can even play movies straight from the QuickTime Movie Player to the handycam.

With a Firewire connection and EchoFire, you won't need a video playback card for your PC. And if you don't like the idea of using your camcorder for this digital bridge, you can buy an inexpensive DV deck for the same purpose. After being connected to a reference monitor, your photos, logos, and DV clips can be seen on analog TV devices and properly previewed as you work in your editing and animation applications.

DESIGN FOR RGB When designing title cards or motion graphics for television work, you've got to consider the limitation of the TV screen. Compared to computer monitors, televisions sets are extremely low-quality displays. They have slightly more than 400 lines of resolution, and images are shown as alternating interlaced fields of information. This tends to create some problems for artwork that normally looks terrific on a PC. For example, using thin horizontal lines in your artwork will undoubtedly produce an excessive flicker, and diagonal lines will appear to stair-step their way around the screen if they are not substantially thick.

So it's important to heed a few warnings. Make sure any lines in your artwork are at least several pixels wide — even thicker if the lines are vertical or diagonal. For the same reason, small text does not appear legible on television. Words that seem crisp and clear on a computer screen will be difficult to read under the constant scanning of standard TV sets. Avoid visual patterns with harsh, saturated colors that are directly adjacent to each other, these intense swatches (especially reds and greens) create oscillations that can be shocking to the human eye. This phenomenon is based on the way the human eye reacts to the phosphorus screen images, especially on cheap or older sets. Level of grays and softer pastoral colors or earthtones (like the dusty tones found in westerns), tend to display quite well on television. Whenever possible, try to create logos and artwork that fall within acceptable palettes of NTSC-safe swatches; you can find filters in many programs, like Photoshop and After Effects, that isolate the best colors for broadcast design elements.

Although computer-generated images seen on an NTSC reference monitor still appear as RGB signals — separated into red, green, and blue channels of information — most artists and designers are accustomed to working within the RYB palette, combining red, yellow, and blue to create their desired colors. (CMYK printing techniques are simply an extension of the RYB color system.) Imagine loading a client's logo onto a new Photoshop canvas and previewing the image on your NTSC reference monitor only to discover that the spot colors of the artwork have no RGB equivalents and cannot be accurately reproduced for TV. For this reason, most designers creating logos for giant international companies always check their colors to ensure that they will look right under Web-friendly and TV-friendly palettes.

A little-known program for reconciling the RYB palette with RGB values is Toolfarm's *ColorTheory*. It's the digital equivalent of a designer's color wheel, that spinning sundial based on the studies of Bauhaus professor Johannes Itten and used by the likes of Andy Warhol and other modernists trained in classical methods. Used by a growing number of contemporary TV and Web artists, ColorTheory transforms Itten's time-tested formulas for proper primary, secondary, tertiary, pastel, neutral, and discordant color schemes into combinations that are just as pleasing when displayed on an NTSC reference monitor. ColorTheory works as a stand-alone application or as a plug-in for Photoshop and After Effects and allows you to import almost any artwork into a window so you can scour among hundreds of tonal variations while viewing the original elements. Effectively, ColorTheory translates all variations of red, yellow, and blue with the closest cousin on NTSC/PAL monitors so that Web and broadcast designers can make their television work look as harmonious as traditional print masterpieces.

But ColorTheory is also great for discovering ideal color combinations, because it can randomize its selections to offer millions of sample swatches. By selecting a color in a frame of video, you can begin to use established theoretical formulas to explore various complements. When creating titles, you can ensure that the color of text against moving video is a sound match by selecting the pixels of a frame and asking the ColorTheory software to suggest a complementary color. By adjusting the settings, ColorTheory will add a number of other suggestions. Even across a changing scene, you can track colors in video and set up a controlled palette of colors based on the footage so the text is never garish or inappropriately contrasting with elements in the background. ColorTheory can also recommend analogous colors, which often introduce better results for the titles across a consistent color backdrop.

KEEP AN EYE ON YOUR LEVELS After you've got a hold on colors, you'll need to watch out for the most extreme levels of luminance, namely black and white. Luminance refers to the amount of light a video signal must process to achieve different shades of color, and each pixel carries its own luminance value. In digital video terms, black is not necessarily the darkest color in your palette, nor is white the brightest. This is due to the fact that luminance in video displayed on a television can differ slightly from the brightness levels in files originating on a computer monitor.

Luminance ranges are problematic for digital filmmakers, particularly those who mix DV footage with animation or motion graphics composited in programs like Adobe After Effects. For example, when creating a title sequence for a movie, you might notice different levels of blackness appearing within the same frame; black borders around vector shapes or converted type may look very black compared to transparent areas, which reveal a different value in the black background. These changes can often occur when you are attempting to integrate stock footage from various sources.

Another scenario where luminance ranges become troublesome is when artists are outputting video footage from different applications to the same tape. For example, an artist might want to build a demo reel with some 3D animations as well as some video editing samples. When exporting a project from the 3D application, there might be a few seconds of black background recorded to the tape after the animation has finished. Then, switching to an editing application, a short movie is recorded to the same tape, with a few seconds of black background in front of the clip. When viewed by the prospective client, the black background may appear to shift between segments for no apparent reason. It can be quite frustrating to see these uneven results, but they are avoidable if you prepare your files correctly.

First of all, you need to understand that almost all computer graphics applications (including image-manipulation software like Photoshop, 3D rendering engines, and compositing programs like After Effects) define black and white values as maximum extremes of brightness. In these programs, black is automatically set to zero percent of brightness, or the RGB color value of 0/0/0. On the other end, white is seen as 100 percent of brightness in an image, represented as the RGB color value of 255/255/255. Together they define a total luminance range from 0 to 255, where no value ever becomes darker than pure black or brighter than pure white.

Most DV footage is captured into computers using a *codec* (a common compression format) that defines brightness in a more limited range of values. Within these video clips, black is considered any value over six percent of brightness, represented by the RGB color value of 16/16/16. This leaves room in the luminance range for values that are darker than the black portions of a video frame.

Why would anyone need a color value that is blacker than black? Well, consider the dark bands that run on the top and bottom of your television screen during a wide-screen presentation of a DVD movie. Those black areas need to be distinguishable from the video inside the letterboxed area, so they are created using values that are even denser than the darkest pixels of a movie.

Conversely, white pixels in digital video are defined as anything greater than 92 percent of full brightness or the RGB color value of 235/235/235. This prevents the occurrence of "hot spots," those superbright areas of video that seem to glow long after the image has left the screen. Most professionals carefully monitor their video shoots to avoid luminance levels that approach pure white. Aesthetically speaking, white is not easy on the eyes; when creating glowing edges or light text, keep the luminance levels just below 92 percent of full brightness. If you have the occasional need to shock an audience with a bolt of lightning or a blinding starburst, you can then dial up the luminance for effect.

The luminance range of 16 to 235 applies to almost all digital video captured over Firewire or Media100 devices and compressed as 8-bit color information. If you are working in a proprietary editing suite that defines video luminance in a range from 0 to 255, you are a lucky dog and free of most luminance problems. And if you are doing straight edits in an application like Apple's iMovie or Adobe

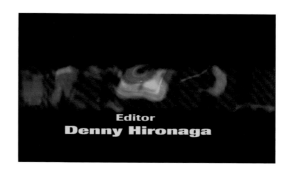

Editor
Denny Hironaga

Premiere, using footage captured from the same camcorder or tape deck — and without adding logos or graphics from other programs — it is unlikely that you will experience shifts in luminance ranges. But most desktop moviemakers combining still images or graphics with motion video will find different luminance levels in their compositions and will have to struggle with these changes.

To correct these inequities, pay attention to mixed media that may have disparate black and white levels throughout your workflow. In most cases, you should leave the luminance ranges of your video footage alone and simply try to match any values in your logos or still photos to the 16 to 235 range when compositing elements together. Using Adobe After Effects, it's easy to make adjustments in luminance: You simply choose Filter, Adjust and apply a Levels filter. In the Effects Controls window, you will see two slider settings to control the Input and Output values of luminance. Once there, you can also enter the range of values with your keypad.

So, you ask, do I adjust the luminance of video clips to match the graphics? Or do I adjust the luminance of graphics to match the video clips? Good question. If you have just one layer of video and only a few layers of graphics in Adobe After Effects, you can leave the video clip unaltered and simply add a filter effect to the other layers, setting only the output values of all graphics to the luminance range of 16 to 235. On the other hand, if you have a complex composition with dozens of layers, you can consolidate your work with an adjustment layer. When using this method, you simply apply the Levels filter to only the adjustment layer, making sure it is placed as the top layer in your composition. However, you must set only the Input levels of luminance to 16 and 235 for any DV clips in the project. This way, when the global changes are made to all layers, the final movie will be rendered with all elements having matching luminance values. With the Expressions features of After Effects 5.0, you can automate these functions to be performed on batches of files or immediately updated to sources as they are replaced in your comps.

There are some gotchas: Be aware that After Effects won't apply changes in luminance to any part of an image that is transparent. This means that if the background color of your composition is set to 0 instead of 16, some areas of your final rendering may appear darker than other black areas. You can remedy this problem by adjusting the background color or by placing a 16-to-235 solid black layer at the very bottom of your composition to make sure transparent elements are backed by proper levels of brightness. Also, watch out for special fades or dissolves that are timed to end when a video background goes to black; if you have automatically set a layer to fade to 0 instead of 16, you may be left with a slightly ghosted image during a few frames. Likewise, if you want to create an effect where the video image seems to burn up and holes appear in the canvas, you may want to leave the composition background blacker than the video black.

Don't be frazzled by all of this black and white nonsense. It's incredibly simple after you have done it once or twice. But apply yourself to understanding its application because it will dramatically improve the professionalism of your reel.

KNOW YOUR ALPHA CHANNELS In broadcast design, the devil is in the details — or more specifically, around the edges. Cheesy video effects are usually given away by the poor integration of foreground objects with their background. That's because the designer didn't take the time to prepare a proper mask, matte, or alpha channel. Each of these helpful techniques can isolate the different layers of a composition and control how those elements can be mixed together. If you plan to create a lot of motion graphics for broadcast design, especially spinning logos and moving text, you should bone up on the properties of alpha channels.

Alpha channels are extra layers of information that travel with a file into video applications and give your computer a mathematical advantage when calculating complex imagery. By gracefully blending the anti-aliased outlines of objects with transparency modes, alpha channels allow text or 3D animations to be seamlessly masked and rendered with video footage. Better yet, alpha channels can be saved with a composition and repurposed endlessly. The sophisticated graphics that appear on screen during televised football games are simply motion graphics with embedded alpha channels that can be reused week after week.

In most applications, any black pixels in an alpha channel are treated as transparent areas and all white pixels are kept completely opaque. Because alpha channels are based on 8-bit pixel information, they can have 256 levels of gray to determine stages of opacity or transparency between black and white. This powerful function allows programs like After Effects to composite one image on top of another, revealing either a harsh stencil or a subtle blending of the two elements. Many of the images and video footage provided by stock libraries will include an alpha channel with every media file so you can begin to fiddle with transparent effects without preparing the footage.

However, once you discover the myriad of creative possibilities you can employ with alpha channels, you'll want to make alpha channels part of every image you design. The process of making an alpha channel in vector illustrations or still pictures is well known to experienced Photoshop users, but there are slight differences between the types compatible for video work. A straight alpha channel stores transparency information separately from RGB channels. This type is the preferred choice among professionals and comes in handy when you intend to change colors as you experiment with motion. A pre-multiplied alpha channel interweaves the transparency information with RGB data on a pixel-hy-pixel basis. This means that colors cannot easily be extracted from the alpha channel without much difficulty. For this reason, pre-multiplied alpha channels often produce distracting colors in the edges of object that expose the effects.

Unfortunately, Photoshop users can inadvertently create pre-multiplied alpha channels if they are not careful to separate their alpha information from RGB colors that tend to sneak into the anti-aliased areas of masked images. Understanding how artwork should be originated to take advantages of alpha channels is beyond the scope of this chapter and better demonstrated within the applications. One of the finest resources available on alpha channels is VideoSyncrasies (Desktop Images), a videotape box set hosted by accomplished broadcast designers Chris and Trish Meyer. Another excellent training series on alpha channels is the work of David Biedny and Bert Monroy, called "Photoshop Inside & Out" (Interactive Digital Intelligence Group). The series dedicates an entire section to "Channels and Masking," an excellent guide to image modes that create complex alpha channels. These training tapes explain the complexities of using alpha channels when compositing 3D art or EPS logos against moving backgrounds and include many other useful insights.

THE ROOSTER DESIGN GROUP ON PRINT

The Rooster Design Group is a design and strategy firm based in New York City. The principals, Fran Gaitanaros and Fernando Music, started the company believing that excellence in design demands cooperation and hands-on participation found in an environment of attentive and invested professionals.

Fran and Fernando come from varied backgrounds, printmaking and architecture, respectively. Their formal training, combined with a passion for seeing an idea realized in its best form — whether that be a printed piece, new media, or a built environment — makes up the Rooster's basic ideology.

Clients range from fields as diverse as art galleries, non-profit organizations, fashion, and financial institutions. And they all keep coming back for more.

The Rooster Design Group has been in business since early 1999. Find out more at: www.theroostergroup.com

IN PRINT — A PRIMER Our culture has become consumed by design on a broad scale, mostly because it seems that anyone with access to a computer has license to say, "I'm a designer." Any investigation would turn up sufficient evidence to support that claim. Your grandmother desktop publishes her church newsletter, your contractor sends you a PDF. Desktop publishing is now for everyone. How fantastic. But as with everything, the more you know, the more you realize you don't know. And design, specifically print design, is no exception.

A BRIEF HISTORY Print design — or design for print — is not without a history. This is a medium that is tactile, has weight, fragrance, and, under the right circumstances, moves you. Having a basic understanding of the process is only the beginning. Print design is, by its very nature, subjective; and applying the "rules" doesn't guarantee that you can create good design. It simply requires thoughtfulness, patience, and practice.

The basic terminology for most desktop-publishing comes from the world of print: cut, copy and paste. Great print designers of the 1940s and '50s such as Lester Beal and Paul Rand championed this style, creating work that was visually arresting — sometimes technically challenging — and always about an idea. There are many schools of thought on design — some subscribe to strict formulas, whereas others may find art in freedom. A modern typographic poster can be as beautiful as a classic Swiss advertisement. On the surface, they may be polar opposites (stylistically), but they can share similar qualities of rhythm, contrast, symmetry, and scale. These qualities transcend time and help put work into the category of great. The end result is always the same: for a design to be good, it has to be about something. In that way, print design is like all other design disciplines. Understanding these ideas can start to give you the ability to evaluate print work, without judgements such as "good" or "bad." That knowledge is valuable, but an instinct and emotional response to graphic design is all you need to practice print design.

What moves someone to design in the first place? Motivation can be found in the most ordinary samples of print design. Take, for example, that movie stub you've held onto or milk container you've been staring at your whole life. What is it about the piece? Is it the size? The paper? Does it trigger a memory? Do you see a value in these items beyond their original function? The notion of good or bad design is irrelevant here — a spontaneous reaction to the type, color, and style is as powerful and valid a force behind the need to design as any. Success will also come from understanding the rules — how to create a file, save an image, or organize a page. There is a right way of doing things. Learning the rules will make your life easier and actually give you more freedom and time to do what you need to do — design.

The best way to illustrate the "how to" behind designing for print is to use this book.

MTIV: CASE STUDY Our objective was to design and produce a 200-plus page book that presented Hillman Curtis' work, process, and inspiration. *MTIV* is a showcase for many ideas that need to be communicated with clarity and within a concise format. Decisions can be difficult when the possibilities are endless. Defining the project goals initially was our roadmap, and it kept us focused throughout the life of the project. In this particular case, the question was: "Have we created a space for the work and influences of Hillman Curtis to communicate through the book?"

Book design has its own unique set of obstacles to overcome: legibility, pacing, and scale to name a few. The design of a book is like editing a broadcast piece because it is experienced over time. A book has to present material in a way that sends the appropriate message page after page — sometimes just copy or just images — and the design has to work within both scenarios. In this way, the composition of single pages is important but also has meaning as part of the larger whole. Also, in a book like this one, the reader doesn't necessarily move from left to right and front to back but moves around and discovers things that pique his interest, taking in material as it appeals to him.

Because a book is meant to be held, the scale, weight, and feel of the paper play as important a part in the design as what appears on its pages. Choosing a paper begins with the uncoated or coated debate. An uncoated sheet has a rough texture or tooth to its surface. Uncoated sheets tend to soak up the ink on press, filling in, printing on the heavy side — ideal for print projects where a representation of the imagery is more important to the design than accuracy of details. Because coated sheets are made with a surface coating (hence the name), they allow for maximum smoothness and ink holdout during the printing process. This means that the ink sits on the surface of the sheet, holding onto details better and allowing more freedom on press — ideal for *MTIV*, where accuracy of imagery is an important element in the design. The paper feels smooth to the touch and varies from glossy to dull to matte. Think of it as the difference between writing with a Sharpie on a paper towel versus a piece of glass — one soaks; one sits.

We tend to be loyal to a specific type of paper or mill… especially when we've had successful results with the sheet in the past. But be aware: paper like any product is specified by brand — a more expensive advertised brand of paper can be comparable in quality to a cheaper brand. Paying more does not always guarantee better results — but please, don't be stingy either.

The best way to become familiar with a paper is through your own research. Collect printed pieces that you like for future reference. They can be presented to your printer as samples of the type of results you want to achieve and aid in making an informed paper choice. We usually pick up to three stocks in case one isn't available or certain restrictions apply. With Hillman's book, our choices were McCoy Velvet, Ikono Dull Satin, and Lustro Dull.

Our next step was to estimate the final page count, size, finishing, and binding options. As we were writing this chapter, this book was "spec-ed" out as soft cover, perfect bound with a matte laminate, which is a plastic film bonded by heat for cover protection. Then we requested a blank unprinted paper dummy. Actual prototypes eliminate any mystery behind the physicality of the final book. Holding the dummies in our hands for the first time created excitement and marked a beginning.

THE DESIGN AND PRODUCTION Finalizing the size or trim of the book is the first step. The second is building the page. We designed *MTIV* on a Mac using QuarkXPress to create the layouts with a combination of Photoshop and Illustrator to manipulate and create artwork — standard industry fare. For the book, we explored the elements, manipulated the grid, and presented our recommendations. Concepts included a chapter opener and three spreads. All aspects of the proposed book design were covered — typography, image treatment, pacing, and palette. There were obvious differences in the approaches and one constant — the use of clean white space as a defining force. Within a week, comments, questions, and adjustments gave way to completed templates with grids.

Templates were created as "master pages" in our Quark files. (Templates function as a grid for specific elements of the book's pages.) Our master pages had grid lines which defined column widths, gutter capacity, folio placement, credit placement, type safety area, trim, stylesheets, and image treatment. We created both left and right pages, together forming a spread. Two colors were selected for the invisible guides: blue for main margins and columns, green for secondary guides. These drawn guides were not meant to box in the design or to force a static hand against the designer. They created structure for the page. (The importance of defining the usage of these elements is that it allows the reader to become familiar with the book's rhythm and function through a certain degree of predictability and repetition.) When a new page was added to our Quark document, it contained these elements, saving us time and ensuring accuracy.

The gutter (Item 1 Figure 1) included the space or inner-margin area where the book was bound. (Because part of the book's pages get lost during

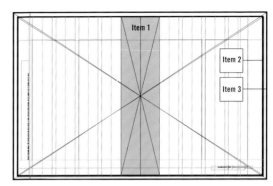

Figure 1

Figure 2

binding, it is important to be sensitive to that area. Don't put text or a face in the gutter if it is meant to be read or seen.) We determined the best binding method based on budget and design aesthetic as perfect bound (a variation of side stitching). The printer determined the minimum safety amount of the gutter. That information was given to us and was not debatable. With *MTIV*, we chose to increase the amount of gutter space, both for additional safety and as part of our design aesthetic of maximum use of white space.

The trim (Item 2 Figure 1) was determined by the final size. (The trim is literally where the page gets cut.) Three sides of the book were trimmed on a guillotine-style cutter. Our trim size was 8 x 20 inches opened, and 8 x 10 inches closed. (Although a cutter is set to cut each sheet the same size, a safety — referred to as bleed — of approximately one-fourth inch outside the trim edge (Item 3 Figure 1) guarantees that type or artwork that bleeds off the edge intentionally isn't unintentionally eliminated.)

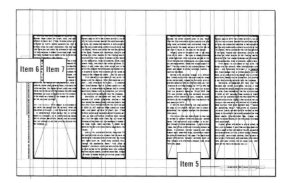

Figure 3

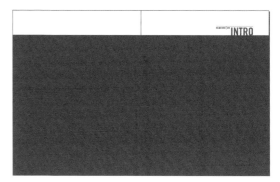

Figure 4

Figure 5

Again, these rules were not debatable. Never decrease the safety amount given to you. Never. When the final amounts of gutter capacity and inner safety were calculated and subtracted from the overall size of the page, we were left with the live area (Item 4 Figure 2), the area for the design.

Imagery plays an important role in the story-telling of the book — the copy is closely informed by photo selection. After spending periods of time with all the potential photographs, we made a selection, asking ourselves, "Does this image support the idea?" Then we called in an outside opinion. That person was asked to either reinforce, confirm, or reject our decisions.

Saving and prepping images is a different story. Unless your printer has given specific image-saving instructions, images for full-color print are generally saved as 260 to 300-dpi (dots per inch, a measure of a printed image), as TIFF or EPS files — unlike images meant to be seen on screen, which are generally saved as 72-dpi RGB files. *MTIV* was printed using the standard four-color process, which consists of cyan, magenta, yellow, and black, so the images and final mechanical files were saved as CMYK.

A hairline black holding rule was applied to the edge of all artwork. We felt that it aided in "grounding" the imagery against the starkness of white space.

Our column size was determined by how large we wanted to present HillmanCurtis.com portfolio pieces. The two-column grid allowed us to tell a story through multiple sequences — eight stills on a page, four fitting within each column, sixteen per spread. In contrast, chapter openers and other imagery were presented large, sometimes crossing the gutter or bleeding off the page. The use of scale helped differentiate between portfolio work and other imagery and effectively allowed more variety within the pages.

TYPE AND TONE The most satisfying and creative solutions stem from equal parts client participation and our own inspired design team. Eventually the solution will begin to reveal itself through group interactions. We make references to Pantone colors or paper to describe the personality and feeling of the piece, as in, "It's 296 — straight out of the tube — pure," or "The brochure has got to feel — Agaramond — classic." This phase works as a character study — a presketching step for us.

We followed that approach with this book, too. *MTIV* just feels Trade Gothic and 1605.

Trade Gothic is legible and unfussy, so it was our initial feeling for the book's design. The face doesn't have any serifs or decorative edges, and its consistent stroke weight feels modern and strong. Trade Gothic doesn't need to be large to be bold and emphasize importance. It works well for headings and smaller credit information. After the readability test, a bit of tweaking and experimentation, the text decision was made: 9 points (the measure used in type) over 12 points leading (space between lines of copy). Folios or page numbers were identified on the lower-right page (Item 5 Figure 3) and credit information ran up the left side in a smaller bolder Trade Gothic (Item 6 Figure 3). We saw those two pieces of information as secondary — meaning we wanted them to be seen or read after the main copy or imagery.

After the typography was finalized, we created style sheets. In Quark, under the Edit menu, we selected Style sheets, selected New, named our style and plugged in the attributes: font, size, leading, color, and so on (Figure 4). (Doing this allows you to bring raw text into your document, and with one selection instantly having that text assume the characteristics defined in your style sheets.)

Since the columns of text worked as beautiful forms (Item 7 Figure 3) alone on a page or spread, we didn't feel forced to find an image to coincide with every thought. In addition, possible uneven column heights allowed for flexibility. A new thought was presented with the start of a new column. Text columns maintained their width throughout the book and started at the same height, mimicking text placement in chapter openers.

Accent colors (Figure 5) for divider pages or text breakers were necessary in the design to break up all the black text and add dimension to the pages.

They felt like the burnt oranges of 1605 or 167 because those colors are bright, bold, and good partners to black text. (Those Pantone colors were re-created as CMYK colors; generally we look at Pantone chips for color inspiration.) But the logic ends there; we just loved the dirtiness of the color and how awesome it looked in one large mass. Used sparingly, it added focus points to the text and dramatically presented a new chapter.

The design of every page of *MTIV* has a story behind it, but we can't tell you anymore beyond this point because as we write, our production deadline is fast approaching (the only outstanding content is our article, bio, and photos). We've completed the first two sections of the book, Process and Inspiration, and are presenting the initial layouts for the Practice section tomorrow. The final pieces to design are the layouts for the dedication, table of contents, works cited, general index, and about the author sections. Our design is well under way; what comes next is the part of the process that often goes overlooked but is as important to the final outcome as the words we choose or the images we create — the file prep and printing.

PREP AND RESPECT Print design is comprised of two parts: the design and the delivery. What distinguishes print work — and influences its impact — is presentation. Great design that is printed poorly is a letdown, as is underwhelming design that is printed beautifully. Design may be subjective, but printing is not: Bad printing detracts from the message.

Eventually, all designers will have their first prepress and printer experience starting a long time before the design stage and concluding a long time after. Ours involved:

- educating our client about the process
- researching paper, color, and materials
- determining print technique and finishing
- determining quantities
- making specs for job estimates
- creating printer dummies
- creating mechanicals

Most print projects and the prepress responsibilities vary, depending on the printer, their facilities, and the budget. Prepping files for *MTIV* involved printing each page of the book at actual size in color. We triple-checked bleeds, copy, and positioning of all layouts, and then marked up the pages. Some of the final artwork needed to be rescanned on big fancy drum scanners for print projects at the publisher's facility. We wrote FPO (for position only) on any imagery that we were not providing as final electronic art and brief but important notes such as: "add more contrast here;" "beware the positioning there;" "this prints as linework;" and so on. Lastly, we sent out the marked-up hard copies to the editorial team and uploaded the final digital assets, (QuarkExpress files, images, and fonts) to Adobe Studio, an on-line project management application.

A good printer will deliver a job as requested, on time and on budget, if your files are organized correctly. A *great* printer will deliver the job, exceeding your expectations, on time and on budget. Respect your printer. Learn about printing. Don't scream at your printer. Participate, ask questions, and collaborate with your printer. Go on press runs. Don't hand off the files and assume you are finished because you haven't yet:

- proofed bluelines
- proofed loose color and matchprints
- gone on the press runs
- co-ordinated print schedules and deliveries

We think of printing as a phase in the design nurtured by a trusting and smart partnership: the same way we collaborate with a client. Projects are successful when we rely on each other.

IT'S PRINTED The design phase of a book trundles on for a long time after all the text has been finalized. With all the design and edit phases, production and printing knowledge, planning and strategy, one thing is consistent at the end of a print project — the final piece materializes with anticipation. It's as if we are seeing it for the very first time.

I BEGIN WITH AN IDEA, AND THEN IT BECOMES SOMETHING ELSE.

PABLO PICASSO

WRITE THE STORY, TAKE OUT ALL THE GOOD LINES, AND SEE IF IT STILL WORKS.

ERNEST HEMINGWAY

OUR ENEMY REALLY ISN'T CAPITALISM, IT'S CYNICISM. THAT'S ONE OF THE THINGS I LEARNED FROM WOODY (GUTHRIE)... NOT TO BE CYNICAL... THAT CYNICISM... IT DESTROYS YOU, IT ROTS YOU AWAY FROM THE INSIDE. SO THAT SENSE OF OPTIMISM AND HUMANITY... WHICH 20 YEARS AGO I WOULD HAVE CALLED SOCIALISM BUT NOW I'LL CALL COMPASSION... YOU KNOW, THAT IDEA IS STILL OUT THERE AND ALIVE AND IF YOU CAN PLUG INTO THAT AND ENCOURAGE THAT IT MAKES IT ALL WORTH WHILE.

THEY ARE NOT PICTURES, I HAVE MADE A PLACE.

MARK ROTHKO

SAY IT CLEARLY, AND YOU MAKE IT BEAUTIFUL NO MATTER WHAT.

BRUCE WEIGL

GOD IS IN THE DETAILS.

LUDWIG MIES VAN DER ROHE

ACKNOWLEDGMENTS A great deal of this book is about the value of collaboration. About how essential the team is to the ultimate success of any given project. It's also about finding your starting points and inspiration in the work of others, and how that is a form of collaboration in itself. It's about the creative path that we all share, and how the work we produce may, in turn, inspire another contemporary or future designer.

So it probably comes as no surprise that the book itself is the product of a rich collaborative effort, on all levels of its development, as much informed by the visions of those involved as my own. So in these two pages, I would like to express my heartfelt thanks and give credit to all those who helped me with *MTIV*.

First, there's Homera J. Chaudhry, who really made this book happen. As the Managing Director at hillmancurtis, inc., Homera truly earns her title with everything she does here. She manages every project we take on, and this book was no exception. In fact, I'll bet it was the most demanding project she's helmed. Homera did everything from setting and maintaining deadlines to managing its content; proofreading; coordinating its design; procuring rights-releases from corporations, artists, and museums; and ultimately, holding the line on the vision behind the book. She worked directly with everyone involved – the designers, editors, myself, etc. – to ensure the highest possible quality on each of those levels. For all of her efforts, on this and every project, I am truly grateful and deeply impressed.

Then there's David Alm. I first met David in early 2001, when he came by the studio to interview me for a feature he was writing for *RES* magazine – incidentally one of my favorite DV magazines. My first impression of him was that he was just way too smart. He was freaking me out at first, but I hung in there, caught up to him and the interview turned into an open and friendly conversation. So a couple of months later, after I'd written a few chapters, I called him up to see if he'd have time to help me better organize my thoughts. From that point on, I handed all my initial drafts over to him, and not only did he make the writing flow much better, he actually added to it, pushing my approach in new directions and expanding the concepts beyond what I'd originally conceived. His input was invaluable and he has since not only helped with a number of other projects, but, as with everyone here, become a very good friend as well.

Next, there's my old friend and co-worker Ian Kovalik. Ian is our creative director, and he's been with the company almost since the beginning. His touch is apparent in just about everything we do, and with this book, he did a little bit of everything. He worked with me in the early stages to determine the book's general topics, and how to best arrange and present them. He also did many of the illustrations in the book, and I relied on his opinions every step of the way, as I do in all of our endeavors. He is a great designer and a joy to work with.

Matt Horn is another contributor to whom I am deeply indebted. Matt worked with us for about two years, during which time he added to this and other projects in so many ways. He prepared most of the book's images for publication, proofread its copy, and managed the delivery of all its files throughout the process.

Grant Collier helped with the early stages of the book's design. And though the final design was done by The Rooster Design Group, his thoughtfulness and creativity resonate throughout its pages.

Which leads me to – who else? – The Rooster Design Group. The small design firm consists of Fernando Music and Fran Gaitanaros, who happen to have been our loft mates during the production of the book – a truly fortuitous convenience. In early 2001, they had to leave their space on the floor beneath ours, and came upstairs to ask if there might be room for them in our office. I remember thinking, Hell no!... Another design company in our space? Forget it! Fortunately, I came to my senses and we have since formed a loose partnership of sorts. They often help us with some of our print jobs. After working with F and F, as we call them, on a few projects, it became clear that they were the ones to really bring the book's design home. Their style and philosophy were a perfect fit for the book. They read the whole thing before forming any ideas and paid careful attention to reflecting its content through its visual layout from start to finish. They worked overtime – and then some – to make it something we could all be proud of for a long, long time. I now count them as not just indispensable design collaborators, but also as close friends.

Joe Lowery is someone I go back with a long way. He helped me write my first book, *Flash Web Design*, and helped me form the idea behind this one. We met a few times at a café and brainstormed. It was from those sessions that the book's outline and title originated, and for that I'm grateful to Joe, as well as for the two chapters he contributed to the "Practice" section.

I also want to thank all of the artists and designers who allowed us to reprint their work. Not only do the pieces add immeasurably to the book's beauty, the process gave me the opportunity to personally contact some of our most revered influences. I hope this book conveys our sincere appreciation and the deep respect we have for their work.

Then there are the eight designers, developers, and industry leaders who leant their expertise to make the "Practice" section the comprehensive guide that it is. Their essays offer dimensions I could never have created alone, and the book is much fuller for them.

And of course, there are my publishers – Steve Weiss and David Dwyer at New Riders. They are truly the freaks of the publishing industry, never satisfied with second-best. We had many moments of stress and friction as we plugged away towards the finished product, but they were worth it. I genuinely appreciate their steadfast determination, even if we sometimes disagreed. They were an indispensable part of the process.

Finally, I want to thank my wife, Christina. She is, and always has been, my most treasured collaborator, someone I run everything by and whose opinion means the world to me.

Oh yeah... Jazzy J, I love you.

CREDITS

PAGE 102
Bill Viola
Still from "Stations" (1994)
Video/sound installation
Collection:
Fdition 1, The Bohen Foundation;
promised gift in honor of Richard E.
Oldenburg to The Museum of Modern
Art, New York
Edition 2, Museum for Contemporary
Art, Zentrum fur Kunst und
Medientechnologie, Karlsruhe
Photo: Kira Perov

PAGE 103
New York, 1998
© Philip-Lorca diCorcia
Courtesy Pace/MacGill Gallery,
New York

PAGE 105
60 Seconds With... Sum 41
Design: hillmancurtis, inc.
©hillmancurtis, inc.

PAGE 106
Divine Inspiration
Shared Inspiration.
©hillmancurtis, inc.

PAGE 109
PICASSO, Pablo. Les Demoiselles
d'Avignon. Paris (June-July 1907) Oil
on canvas, 8' X 7' 8" (243.9 x 233.7
cm). The Museum of Modern Art, New
York. Acquired through the Lillie P.
Bliss Bequest. Photograph © 2002
The Museum of Modern Art, New York.

PAGE 110
Le bonheur de vivre, Henri Matisse,
BF #719 © 2002 Reproduced with
the permission of The Barnes
Foundation ™ All Rights Reserved.

PAGE 111
Tracer. Robert Rauschenberg
The Nelson-Atkins Museum of Art,
Kansas City, Missouri (Purchase)
F84-70

PAGE 114
No Way Out Billboard by Paul Rand
The Paul Rand Collection
Yale University Library

PAGE 114
Anatomy of a Murder. Saul Bass
The Kobal Collection

PAGE 116
Josef Müller-Brockmann. Zürich
Tonhalle, Poster 'musica viva'. 1958
© pro litteris, Zürich, © 2002 Artists
Rights Society (ARS), New York/Pro
Litteris, Zürich

PAGE 116
Josef Müller-Brockmann.
Book-jacket, 'The Graphic Artist and
his Design Problems'. 1st edition,
Verlag Arthur Niggli, Teufen, 1961 ©
pro litteris, Zürich © 2002 Artists
Rights Society (ARS), New York/Pro
Litteris, Zürich

PAGE 117
hillmancurtis Web site Grid Structure.
©hillmancurtis, inc.

PAGE 118
Colors #13. Tibor Kalman
© Colors Archive

PAGE 119
Lucent Technology Center for the
Performing Arts (NJPAC)
Design: Paula Scher, Rion Byrd,
Pok Chow
Photograph: © Peter Mauss/Esto.

PAGE 120
IKKO TANAKA. NOH PLAY "THE 5TH
KANZE NOH" (1958) © Ikko Tanaka
Design Studio

PAGE 121
Barbara Kruger
Untitled (It's a Small World But Not If
You Have To Clean It). 1990
Photographic silkscreen on vinyl
143 x 103 in.
The Museum of Contemporary Art,
Los Angeles
Purchased with funds provided by
the National Endowment for the
Arts, a Federal Agency, and
Douglas S. Cramer.

PAGES 122-123
Stills from "Stop Making Sense"
(1984)
Title Design: Pablo Ferro
A film by Jonathan Demme
& Talking Heads
Courtesy: Pablo Ferro

PAGE 125
Screenshots of the one9ine site
Site design and development: one9ine
Work by Matt Owens

PAGE 126
Stills from Soulbath.com
Design: Hi-Res! London

PAGE 126
Video stills from the film *Newport*
Design: David Hartt and
Gary Breslin

PAGE 127
Screenshots from the miniml.com site
Design: Craig Kroeger
© 2001 miniml.com

PAGE 127
Stills from FAKTUR/A
Design: Kontruktiv.net
© Matt Anderson 2002

PAGE 128
Adobe Studio Motion Brand comps
Design: hillmancurtis, inc.
© 2001 Adobe Systems Incorporated.
All rights reserved. Adobe, Acrobat,
After Effects, GoLive, Illustrator,
InDesign, LiveMotion, PageMaker,
Photoshop, and Premiere is/are either
[a] registered trademark(s) of Adobe
Systems Incorporated in the United
States and/or other countries.

PAGE 129
Final Adobe Studio Brand
Design: hillmancurtis, inc.
© 2001 Adobe Systems Incorporated.
All rights reserved. Adobe, Acrobat,
After Effects, GoLive, Illustrator,
InDesign, LiveMotion, PageMaker,
Photoshop, and Premiere is/are either
registered trademark(s) of Adobe
Systems Incorporated in the United
States and/or other countries.

PAGE 130
Anything That Moves.
©hillmancurtis, inc.

PAGE 133
Rothko, Mark. Untitled. Gift of The
Mark Rothko Foundation, Inc.,
Photograph © 2001 Board of
Trustees, National Gallery of
Art, Washington.

PAGE 139
Hillman at Commercial Shoot
for Hallmark
Photograph: Jeff Lipsky
©Jeff Lipsky

PAGE 143
Cover, from TAYLOR'S GUIDE TO
ORCHIDS. Copyright © 1996 by Judy
White. Reprinted by permission
of Houghton Mifflin Company.
All rights reserved.

PAGE 144
Detail from MetaDesign Website
Design: MetaDesign Design Staff

PAGE 149
Color wheel illustration courtesy
of Grafix Press, Ltd. Previously
published by PANTONE ® GUIDE
TO COMMUNICATION WITH COLOR
by Leatrice Eiseman.

PAGES 186-197
Chapter reprinted from *Don't Make Me
Think! A Common Sense Approach to
Web Usability* (New Riders)
www.stevekrug.com

INSIDE BACK COVER
Photo by Brigham Field

INDEX